A HUMBLE GUIDE
TO FIXING
EVERYTHING IN
BRAND, MARKETING,
AND SALES
BY BRET STARR

Praise for *A Humble Guide to Fixing Everything in Brand, Marketing, and Sales*

"Great brands are built with great intention. Bret gets this in ways CEOs and Boards should heed. Building great brands and designing great experiences go hand in hand. It's painfully obvious *what doesn't work*. Through the lenses of experience and brand, Bret shows us in this book *what does*."
—*Henry Albrecht, Limeade CEO and Work Tech Pioneer*

"Bret's book is a manifesto for the disillusioned marketer. I picked it up to give the first few pages the sniff test and didn't put it down until I was finished. Finally, a book on sales and marketing in tech that's not out of date next week."
—*Michael Carden, Co-CEO and Co-Founder, Joyous*

"Work Tech expert and Starr Conspiracy Founder and CEO Bret Starr delves deep into the interconnected worlds of marketing and customer experience, revealing the art and science behind crafting unforgettable journeys. Packed with insightful strategies that disrupt the norm, it is a must-read for marketers, C-suite leaders, and aspiring founders alike, empowering them to orchestrate success through the symphony of customer-centricity across their businesses."
—*Julie D. Knight, Chief Marketing Officer, Unit4*

"Bret is one of the best inside/outside-of-the-box thinkers I've ever met. His exceptional ability to clearly articulate why businesses must intentionally design and deliver differentiated customer experiences makes this book a must-read."
—*Patrick Manzo, CEO, WorkTango*

Bret Starr
A Humble Guide to Fixing Everything in Brand,
Marketing, and Sales
© 2023, Bret Starr

CONTENTS

A defining moment is a point in time in which a person comes to believe that the true and essential nature of a thing has been revealed.

If you must blink, do it now. Pay careful attention to everything you see and hear, no matter how unusual it may seem. And please be warned: If you fidget, if you look away, if you forget any part of what I tell you—even for an instant—then our hero will surely perish.

—Kubo and the Two Strings

CHAPTER 1

Why Your Marketing Shit Is Broken

The blocking and tackling era is over and the road to hell is paved with performance optimizations.

I have a story to tell you. So please be patient with me.

Maybe you're reading this book because your best marketing stuff isn't working the way it used to. Maybe your company is a market leader in search of a badly needed turnaround. Maybe you're a highflier, but things have slowed down over the past year or so and you're looking for a new spark. Maybe you're a plucky bootstrapper who senses an opportunity to make gains against market leaders, but you're struggling to find the magic formula in sales and marketing. Or maybe you're new to the tech market and are overwhelmed by the go-to-market landscape.

First of all, I want you to know that you're not alone. Nearly every tech company I talk to is experiencing performance declines from their tried-and-true sales and marketing strategies—the stuff that used to work really well. Many don't know why. Is it the economy? Is it a pandemic hangover? Is it internal execution? They may not know what's causing it, but they know what it looks like. Here are a few of the complaints that I hear literally every day:

- Sales and marketing cost is increasing
- Performance is declining
- Lead volume is going down
- Lead quality is getting worse
- Sales conversion is low
- Customer satisfaction is declining
- Churn is high

While many don't know why their sales and marketing is in a slump, some others have a general idea about the root cause of the problem. *But they don't know what to do about it.* And each new thing they try deepens their frustration with the current state of their sales and marketing performance.

Were marketing people fired? Was sales leadership replaced? Get a new CEO? Did you rebrand? Did you shift strategies and models? Change your message? Implement new martech? Build a new website? Switch agencies? Launch new products? Shift budgets? Bring people back to the office? Send them back home?

And none of it has worked. Or, at least, it hasn't brought you to the promised land.

What if I told you that I know why your sales and marketing shit is broken? And what if I told you that I know how to fix it? *Would you believe me?* And then what if I proceeded to tell you exactly what to do about it?

Well, that's what I do in this book. And it will probably scare the hell out of you. Because what I'm here to tell you is that the way we used to do things in sales and marketing—the way most of us are doing things now—just doesn't work anymore. The blocking and tackling era is over and the road to hell is paved with performance optimizations.

And when you're finished reading this book, even if I have shaken you to the core, you still may not believe me. But when the Big Tech go-to-market machinery finally breaks down for good, at least you'll have this alternative theory of sales and marketing to fall back on. And that's worth a few hours of your time, isn't it?

I guess we'll see.

CHAPTER 2

Big Picture

When I wrote this book, I broke the script.

I've thought a lot over the past year or so about how to tell this story. On the one hand, it's a very simple story—I have the answers to some very big questions. On the other hand, it's a little more complex because getting to the answers requires a shift in context that, by necessity, changes the questions that should be asked. Here are the types of questions that get asked all the time:

- What's wrong with our sales and marketing stuff?
- How can I improve the things we're doing?

Questions like these lead us to pursue performance optimizations from our current people, processes, and technology. They are firmly rooted in a critical evaluation of how we make better the things we're doing now. But the more important questions are the ones that would cause us to critically evaluate the efficacy of the things themselves, rather than how we're doing them. These questions do not lead us down the narrow path of performance optimizations to drive incremental improvements—they lead us to devise new ways of doing things that result in innovative approaches and transformational outcomes. And *these* questions aren't being asked frequently enough:

- **What's wrong with the *state* of sales and marketing?**

- **What should we *all* be doing differently?**

Like I said, I have the answers to these questions—those frequently asked and those not asked frequently enough. So why don't I just tell you right now and be done with it? I considered that very approach, actually. Originally, I was going to start like this:

Across the tech industry, sales and marketing performance is in decline. Here's how to fix it:

- Bam

- Pow

- Whammy

- *Mic drop*

But that approach wouldn't work. Why? Precisely because the most important answers I have are to questions that are rarely asked. And what I've found is that it takes a lot of storytelling and convincing to get most people to the point of agreeing that not only do we need to ask different questions, but that the answers are both urgent and overdue.

So if I started with the answers, most people would dismiss them immediately. Because most people don't think they need a completely different approach to sales and marketing. What most people think they need are performance optimizations to their existing approach.

The Script for Business Books

There is a script for business books, you know? I have a part and you have a part. Your role is that of the discriminating reader. You're only supposed to buy this book if someone tells you about it or if it shows up on some list somewhere. And if you *do* buy it, you are supposed to skip the front matter entirely, scan the table of contents, and maybe read a few pages from a chapter that piques your interest, all the while judging whether the book is worth reading from start to finish. And my role in the script is that of the dedicated author. I'm supposed to consider the book's position and marketability, carefully plan the structure, commit to a disciplined writing process over the course of months or years, and polish the manuscript until my fingers bleed, resulting in an end product that is concise, easy to read, and practical in scope. *Or hire a ghostwriter.*

When I wrote this book, I broke the script. I am not a dedicated author. I'm an agency founder and CEO. I have work to do for my clients, my people, and my shareholders. So instead of taking some sort of writing sabbatical, I wrote the first draft of this book in two days (it poured out of me). I broke the rules for front matter, spreading the preface out over the first four chapters and dropping a dedication in the middle as its own chapter. And the book is anything but concise, easy to read, and practical in scope. I ramble. I go on a lot of tangents. I switch back and forth between topics. And I tell a bunch of stories that may not seem absolutely necessary or relevant. *Obviously, I did not hire a ghostwriter.*

I ignored my part in the script. I hope you do the same. I *am* sorry if reading this book is a frustrating experience. All I ask is that you be patient and suspend judgment. Because I believe you'll find the experience valuable in the end.

Many people who read an advance copy of the manuscript for this book told me it had a way of growing in their mind. For most, there was a lightbulb moment. It happened at different points in the book for different people—and for some the moment was weeks after finishing it. But after that lightbulb moment, they couldn't help but see the solutions I present here in nearly every sales and marketing situation they encountered thereafter. So try to suspend judgment while you read and maybe even for a few days after you finish. Be patient. Give me the benefit of the doubt. And then, you tell me if these were questions worth asking and answers worth sharing.

CHAPTER 3

The End of the Blocking and Tackling Era

We are all fine-tuning stock machinery.

I'll jump straight to the punchline. The blocking and tackling era in sales and marketing is over. *But what the hell does that even mean? (Reads Wikipedia.)*

Blocking and tackling is a frequently used idiom in business. It's a reference to American football. The players on the field who do the blocking and the tackling have the least glamorous positions, but their (often unheralded) efforts are critical to the success of the team. And so, in business, blocking and tackling is meant to refer to the basic and fundamental people, processes, and technologies critical to the operation of the company.

In the context of sales and marketing, blocking and tackling refers to the basic and fundamental building blocks we've all come to expect in a tech company. Everyone should have a go-to-market strategy. Everyone should have a marketing model. Everyone should have a sales process. A message framework. An ICP. Digital marketers. SDRs. A martech stack. A sales tech stack. A demand generation strategy. Paid media program. Public relations. Analyst relations. Social media.

Ironically, for the last decade or so, blocking and tackling has been celebrated as anything but. In other words, most companies have come to perceive their blocking and tackling as their primary go-to-market advantage rather than the quiet work that creates a foundation for go-to-market advantage. I want to be very clear on this point: Blocking and tackling is absolutely critical. *But it no longer creates an advantage.*

The Playbook

In the old days (which most of us are still living in), the prevailing perception was that excellence in sales and marketing flowed from a precisely implemented playbook that was constantly optimized. Define the models and processes. Inbound marketing. Outbound sales. MQLs and SQLs. Conversion rates. Salesforce. Marketing automation. Digital marketing.

Back then, simply having such a playbook was an advantage. Hotshots arrived at companies with their playbooks tucked under their arms, ready to demystify the increasingly complex world of tech sales and marketing. These were the original adopters of the modern sales and marketing tech stacks and they were pioneers on the digital frontier. They knew ways and means that other people did not. And when their beautiful, secretive machines were up and running, they crushed the competition with brute-force execution.

I know, because I was one of them.

Later, when nearly everyone had implemented the core elements of the playbook, advantage could be maintained by going deeper. I see your HubSpot and raise you an Outreach. Your inbound campaigns are cute—but check out my ABM strategy. You're still asking BANT questions in the sales process? Let me tell you about purchase intent data.

At some point, the perceived quality of our sales and marketing efforts boiled down to the acronyms we used and the number of sales and marketing tech solutions we owned. I frequently meet with companies that have more than 40 sales and martech solutions. And after careful scrutiny, it turns out the company is paying for many more solutions that aren't even used anymore because they've been forgotten.

These days, everyone has everything. They have the people and the processes and more technology than they know what to do with. They are constantly searching for the next addition to their blocking and tackling machines that will produce even a small advantage. Ask a sales leader about Gong or a marketing leader about ChatGPT and watch their eyes light up.

In the era of blocking and tackling, our mantra has become performance optimization. A little tweak to our process here, a little new tech there. Shave a couple of steps off this click path. Add a point to that conversion rate. Replace a few SDRs. Tighten up the ad groups.

But I'm here to tell you, once more, that the road to hell is paved with performance optimizations. We have reached the point of diminishing returns. We spend more money and more time each year trying to eke out increasingly smaller performance improvements. Meanwhile, costs keep going up and performance keeps going down. In most cases, people aren't asking for innovative go-to-market strategies— they just want more budget to make their existing strategies perform marginally better.

Question the Model

What I find interesting is that all of us are obsessed with improving every aspect of our models, but very few of us are equally obsessed with questioning the models themselves. You know what I mean? I'll elaborate with the following example.

I recently worked with a company to improve their sales and marketing results. Like most companies, they were constantly searching for competitive advantage through performance optimizations to their existing blocking and tackling. In this particular case, they were obsessed with improving their sales conversion rate, which had been in decline for the last year or so. They had come to the conclusion that part of the solution could be found in using purchase intent data to evaluate and prioritize sales opportunities. In fact, the company had recently doubled down on purchase intent by implementing and integrating a popular account-based marketing (ABM) system from a martech vendor known to be a leader in the field of purchase intent solutions. Like all of these systems, this one promises to alert your sales team when a target account tilts into active buyer behavior.

Let's evaluate the assumptions inherent in this initiative. First, the company assumed that the primary and best use of sales effort was in the pursuit of qualified contacts in target accounts that were actively evaluating solutions in their category. Second, the company assumed that any process or solution that provides more accurate and timely data about the purchase intent in target accounts would deliver a competitive advantage. Both of these assumptions were rooted in the conventional wisdom of performance optimization within the prevailing blocking and tackling models of sales and marketing.

But here's an interesting thing that happened. I was reviewing win-loss data with this company. As they were going through the list of competitors they lose to most often, I heard something that struck me as odd. They were losing a lot of deals to one particular competitor in a volume that didn't track with market dynamics.

The competitor they were losing to most was the market leader in their category—no surprise there:

New segment revenue most often gets distributed along the lines of existing market share. In other words, if there are 100 deals closed in your category this month, about 30 of those deals will go to the company with 30% market share, 15 deals will go to the company with 15% market share, and so on. That's true, by the way. Market share order rarely shifts between companies once the market is firmly established. And when it does, it happens slowly and by degrees. It's part and parcel of the primary issue with blocking-and-tackling-as-a-strategy. If everyone is doing the same things as everyone else, why would market share order change?

But the competitor they were losing to second most (and almost as frequently) was a smaller bootstrapped vendor with only a sliver of market share. Why was this happening? Conventional wisdom would have classified this bootstrapped competitor as a major threat. And, in fact, that's exactly what happened. The company was so threatened by this small, bootstrapped competitor (who, by the way, has been around for like *forever* and has been slowly losing market share for years) that they mobilized a team to pore over the competitor's sales, marketing, and product strategy. They spun up endless sales enablement tools aimed squarely at this competitor. Their fear of the competitor even caused them to make significant changes to things like their brand message and website.

But in this case, conventional wisdom was wrong. This laggard competitor wasn't winning a disproportionate share of deals because of their inherent competitive power—they weren't surging in market share. The threat was caused by the company's own misguided attempts to optimize the performance of their blocking and tackling.

Here is what was really happening. The company had an outbound sales model. They had tuned their model to purchase intent. Thus, they were constantly looking for any optimization that would provide them with a purchase intent advantage. In their quest for a competitive advantage in this area, they bought what they believed to be the best purchase intent–driven ABM solution available.

The problem is that the little bootstrapped competitor had purchased the same system. Therefore, the two companies were being notified about purchase intent in the same target accounts at the same time, resulting in an artificially high occurrence of bake-offs. And more head-to-head battles with the same competitor (relative to others) meant more losses to that competitor.

This absurd scenario was generating a distorted signal about the overall market significance of the bootstrapped competitor. And based on that distorted signal, the company had made all kinds of upstream and downstream tweaks to their blocking and tackling aimed directly at a company that should have otherwise been considered a minor threat.

The company started this journey into madness because they were suffering from a declining close rate in sales. They thought they could fix that problem by optimizing their existing sales process with even better purchase intent data. But they were actually making it worse by narrowing their focus on the same target accounts as at least one of their competitors (and probably more).

So back to my point. Instead of obsessing over optimizations to a model that everyone else is using, why weren't they questioning the model itself? As they continued to pursue more timely and accurate purchase intent data with no improvement to close rates, why didn't they stop to ask if purchase intent was a good organizing principle for their sales outreach to begin with? Simply put, it's because purchase intent data has become a generally accepted page in the blocking and tackling playbook. The better solution (which the company has now implemented, resulting in a positive impact on sales conversion) was to back off of purchase intent as the organizing principle for sales outreach. Instead, the company now prioritizes sales outreach based on the combined presence of *engagement* and purchase intent. When both components are not present, the company prioritizes engagement *over* purchase intent. Because in target accounts that signal purchase intent but that have no engagement with your company, it's very likely that one of your competitors has already established an engagement advantage. But in accounts where there's engagement with no purchase intent, one can always focus on deepening engagement and catalyzing purchase intent, so you're positioned as the early preferred vendor. Personally, I would even prioritize target accounts with no engagement and no purchase intent over companies with purchase intent but no engagement.

I see similar scenarios play out in the brand, marketing, and sales experience all the time. Companies focus so much on gaining competitive advantage through performance optimizations to their blocking and tackling that they end up fighting for inches instead of yards. In many ways, we are all fine-tuning stock machinery. We have truly reached the point of diminishing returns. And without significant changes to our mindset about sales and marketing, costs will continue to increase as performance continues to decline.

Technological Determinism and Process Assimilation

When did marketing become more about doing the same things a little better than everyone else and less about doing different things that set us apart? *I know the answer to that, actually (he says, absently adjusting his glasses).* The cause is rooted in technological determinism or the notion that technological innovations have unintended consequences beyond their intended scope. The current state of sales and marketing in the tech sector is a direct result of the introduction of Software-as-a-Service solutions. That incredible technological innovation meant that everyone would have access to relatively cheap customer relationship management (CRM) systems. And as much as the vendors of those systems loved to promote their endless points of differentiation, the truth is that every major sales and martech system (then and now) was based on the same linear customer acquisition model. A funnel. A pipeline. A journey. Therefore, inside every cereal box was a surprise gift of process (and culture) assimilation. And so around the turn of the century, we all began a migration toward sameness.

So why is your sales and marketing shit broken? Why are you forced to spend more each year on eroding results? Let me spell it out:

- Everyone is using the same blocking and tackling strategies
- More companies are spending more money in the same ways
- That puts upward cost pressure on inventory-restrained media (why does a click cost so much?)
- And downward pressure on performance

And all the while, the poor customers (remember them?) have become the target of more sales and marketing nags in a single day than they used to experience in an entire month—or more. Think people out there are muting us? *You betcha.*

CHAPTER 4

I'm Going to Tell You Exactly What to Do

My whole life is wrapped up in this solution.

Can you smell what The Rock is cooking? Blocking and tackling is necessary, but not sufficient. So what are we supposed to do about it?

Before I dive into the solution for this very real problem, I want to be perfectly clear about something. Because this is the part of my message that people often don't hear. I say it. I've already said it here multiple times! But many don't hear it. *Blocking and tackling is critical.* It's necessary. And being good at it is super-important. I'm not saying that we should all kill our martech stacks. I'm not saying that companies should stop engaging in ABM. I'm not saying that we should all stop creating nurture streams or outbound sales cadences. All of these things are critically important.

It's just that these things aren't a strategy in and of themselves. And to be honest, even the best blocking and tackling these days produces some pretty lackluster results.

Blocking and tackling is *not* a strategy. It does not provide an advantage over competitors in a world where everyone has all the same kinds of people, processes, and technology. Blocking and tackling does, however, provide a foundation upon which your go-to-market advantage may be built. But to truly set ourselves apart from competitors, we have to do more. We have to *be* more. We have to create something that is unique to our company and cannot be duplicated.

We have to break the script.

Here's the part where I start telling you exactly what to do. And you're probably not going to like it. Some will probably think I'm just making shit up to sell my agency's services. Others may feel that I'm repackaging old ideas in a new wrapper. And a few might feel that what I'm suggesting is too disruptive, ambitious, or ambiguous to actually be implemented. But here is the honest truth: My whole life is wrapped up in this solution.

I founded The Starr Conspiracy, an experience agency, more than 20 years ago. It's not just a job for me. And it's way more than just some company I started. It's even more than my life's work. *The Starr Conspiracy is my obsession.* Like any obsession, it is equal parts light and dark. It exhilarates and torments me in equal measure. Because the models and strategies I am compelled to create have real-life consequences for people I love. When I am successful, the people around me flourish. My colleagues succeed. Our clients succeed. But when I fail, it means that people around me suffer the consequences.

The last three years or so have been humbling. I've been to the mountain's peak and I've languished in the cold shadows of the valley. Like so many people, I've experienced the massive disequilibrium of having nearly every aspect of my life disrupted and every pillar of my belief system challenged. But this has also been a period of great reflection, level setting, and learning. And so what I'm now about to share with you is something I truly believe. And I wouldn't make such disruptive recommendations casually. There is too much riding on it.

In truth, I've seen the writing on the wall for a while now. But it really took the experiences of the last three years to move me into action. I've sensed and observed the gradual-then-sudden decline of sales and marketing vision and strategy in tech for years. There are more tech companies today than ever before. More money is being spent on sales and marketing each year. Everyone is doing the same stuff. Breakout performances are becoming more rare. And there is an observable lack of innovative sales and marketing models put forward to challenge the status quo. What other conclusion can be drawn? Disruption to prevailing sales and marketing strategies is inevitable, necessary, and desirable.

But what's next?

If I don't answer that question, who will? I'm dead serious about that. It may sound grandiose, but who the hell is going to do something about this mess? I've been yelling about it from the sidelines for the last few years. But I can no longer stand by and do nothing.

I mean, when you really think about it, when was the last time someone shared with you a fundamentally different approach to sales and marketing? I'm not talking about one of those one-shot-business-book fads. I'm talking about a well-reasoned and strongly supported argument for a completely new way of doing things?

Well here's one for ya.

CHAPTER 5

A New Interpretation of Customer Experience

No one can successfully lead sales or marketing anymore (or even companies) without deeply understanding the interdependent relationship between brand, marketing, sales, product, and customer success, and without becoming an expert in strategies that place brand, marketing, and sales in the holistic context of customer experience.

The solution to the current state of sales and marketing is a holistic customer experience. Now, I know how that sounds. I know what you're thinking: *Wait a minute! Customer experience has been around for a while. I thought you were going to bring something new to the table.*

I am. Trust me.

First of all, does anyone actually know what customer experience is? Based on my experience (no pun intended), I can say with great confidence that no one can really provide a satisfying definition of customer experience. And certainly not a compelling one. The reason for the lack of a clear and satisfying definition for customer experience is that it doesn't really mean any singular thing to most people. It means many different things to many different people. And so a lot of folks who are looking for a new framework to achieve brand, marketing, or sales breakthroughs end up nibbling around the edges of customer experience, but most end up dissatisfied. And almost everyone comes to the conclusion that customer experience is not an actionable go-to-market concept. It ends up feeling like something *other* than sales and marketing. Like something that has more to do with product and customer success.

So I'm not going to try to explain customer experience to you as if it were some solid, tangible concept that you just haven't gained a purchase on yet. Rather, I'm laying claim to a new interpretation of customer experience by expanding the scope of previous concepts and by providing a clear definition and a framework for customer experience that can be implemented by tech companies to gain a durable competitive advantage—an advantage that cannot be replicated by competitors, *even if they are using the same framework.* And this framework is additive to the blocking and tackling you've already implemented. It doesn't replace it. *It makes it work better.*

Implicit in my definition of, and framework for, customer experience is a dramatic broadening of the scope traditionally implied by different strategies labeled as customer experience. This framework is holistic. That is to say, it emphasizes the importance of the whole (customer experience) and the interdependence of all its parts (brand, marketing, sales, product, and customer success). Taken to the extreme, it's my humble attempt to fix everything in brand, marketing, and sales—to explain how everything in a tech company fits together, culminating in different degrees of success or failure.

To anchor the thesis of my broader body of work in experience within the specific scope of this book (which is primarily focused on the brand, marketing, and sales experiences created by B2B tech companies), I'll simply say this—no one can successfully lead sales or marketing efforts anymore (or even companies) without deeply understanding the interdependent relationship between brand, marketing, sales, product, and customer success, and without becoming an expert in strategies that place brand, marketing, and sales in the holistic context of customer experience.

CHAPTER 6

A Definition for Customer Experience

Customer experience is the perception of the quality of time spent with a company.

So let's start with a new definition for customer experience. To reiterate, I'm not suggesting that this is a definition that seeks to explain pre-existing notions of customer experience in a different and better way. This is a new definition that lays claim to a broader scope and framework for customer experience. So when I say "customer experience," here is exactly what I'm talking about:

Customer experience is the perception of the quality of time spent with a company.

That's it. But don't kid yourself. *There's a lot there.*

First, customer experience is a **perception** of the quality of time. It's not a fact. It's a subjective opinion about a person's experience with a company based on the interactions they have with the people, places, and things associated with the company. The most important thing to remember is that, since it's a perception, it can be shaped, influenced, and even changed.

Second, it's a perception of the **quality** of time. In this context, quality doesn't mean good or bad, valuable or not valuable. It *could* mean that. But more broadly, it refers to the *essential nature and defining characteristics* of the moments in time experienced with a company. Best to think about it in these terms—how do you feel about a company and how does a company make you feel?

Finally, it's a perception of the quality of **time.** Experiences are formed by hundreds and thousands of moments over big chunks of time. But, as I'll describe later in this book, not every moment has the same power. Some are *defining moments* that end up dominating perceptions, while other moments (the everyday kinds of moments) end up playing a subtle supporting role. People can have a very sharp reaction to any one specific moment. But over time, most everyday moments soften and recede while the overall experience becomes predominantly characterized by a few defining moments.

So when I say "customer experience," I mean the perception of the quality of time spent with a company. The whole company. And any person, place, or thing associated with the company. And for the scope of this book, I mean the overall perception based on the consistent quality of *defining moments* in brand, marketing, sales, product, and customer success.

I'm not using customer experience as a strategic euphemism for customer success. Nor am I characterizing customer experience solely as the sum of interactions that people have with a company's product. And I'm not talking about a mashup of product experience and customer success. Finally, I'm not talking about some abstract creative marketing concept. To put a fine point on it, customer experience is composed primarily of defining moments in the brand experience, marketing experience, sales experience, product experience, and customer success.

This is a new definition of customer experience. I'm talking about a single person's perception of the quality of time spent with your company. And this definition considers every domain in your company. And understanding this definition along with its implied scope and holistic nature is key to escaping the blocking and tackling era as a category leader with a durable go-to-market advantage.

CHAPTER 7

The Purpose of Customer Experience Design

The purpose of customer experience design is to build vendor preference.

So why is a definition for customer experience important? Specifically, why is the definition offered in the last chapter important? *Customer experience is the perception of the quality of time spent with a company.* Because this definition establishes the scope and motivation of the concepts and framework presented in this book. Said another way, the definition establishes the business purpose for customer experience design.

Customer experience is a perception. Since perceptions are subjective, does it not stand to reason that we have the ability to shape them? And perceptions are established over time based on the quality and consistency of moments spent with a company. So does it not stand to reason that the best way to shape perception is to take control of the quality and consistency of moments? To design moments with intention?

If the benefit of shaping perception over time is not obvious, let me state it clearly: It's merely perception that causes people to favor one vendor over another. People build preference for vendors based on their different experiences with different companies over time. So if we can shape the perception of the quality of time spent with our company, then we can build preference for our company in the minds of customers. Vendor preference can have many manifestations, and they are not all confined to traditional notions of brand preference:

- **Brand Preference:** Customers are more likely to recognize your brand, to comprehend its functional associations, and to experience attraction to your brand attributes.

- **Marketing Preference:** Customers are more willing to connect with your company and engage with marketing campaigns, resulting in higher conversion rates across the board.

- **Sales Preference:** Customers are more likely to connect with salespeople, engage with the sales experience, designate you as an early preferred vendor, buy faster, and pay more.

- **Product Preference:** Customers are more likely to deeply engage with your product, expand use, and identify new use cases.

- **Customer Success Preference:** Customers are more likely to provide feedback, buy more products, renew, and promote your company to prospective customers.

The purpose of customer experience design is to build vendor preference. We achieve this goal by creating moments that shape people's perception of the essential nature and defining characteristics of our company (people, places, and things). Our success in shaping people's perception comes down to two factors: (1) the quality of the moments we create and (2) the consistency of defining moments across the entire experience.

When it comes to the quality of moments we create, it's not enough to simply strive for *great* moments that add up to a *great* experience. Two companies competing for the same customer can both create *great* customer experiences, but only one of them can win the customer. This is the problem with approaches to customer experience that are based solely on quantitative metrics. A company can perform well on traditional measures of customer experience such as brand awareness, marketing engagement, sales performance, customer effort score, product engagement, customer satisfaction, and churn, and still not be the vendor preferred by the largest share of the market. The type of customer experience we want to create must be well defined and differentiated from competitors. It must speak to the essential nature and defining characteristics of our company in all its forms. When a buyer says, "Both companies are great, but I chose you because ..." we want to be in control of the *because*.

But carefully defining the quality of the moments and experience we want to create is not enough. We must also *deliver* on the experience consistently. If the *quality* of the experience may be described as the essential nature and defining characteristics of the experience, it should be abundantly clear that people will only arrive at the desired perception of that quality if they actually experience it time and time again. For example, it's hard for me to draw a definitive conclusion about a person's essential nature and defining characteristics if I experience something different every time I interact with them. If they are sometimes helpful and sometimes selfish, sometimes nice and sometimes mean, sometimes this and sometimes that, the only conclusion I may be able to draw is that the person is flaky, unpredictable, or unknowable. But if a person is consistently there for me when I need them, and especially in moments when I need them most (like showing up with a truck on moving day), I am likely to draw the conclusion that the person is dependable. And I will hold on to the perception that they are dependable even if they aren't there for me in a few small moments down the road. But if they're not there for me in a really big moment, or if they've just stopped showing up altogether, in moments big and small, my perception of that person will change. Companies have to show up with the same essential nature and defining characteristics—and the same level of quality—over and over again in multiple moments across the customer experience in order to cement the perceptions that lead to vendor preference—especially in the big moments.

I can't emphasize this last point enough. So many issues in sales and marketing are based almost exclusively on breaks in continuity in the customer experience. Marketing builds one set of perceptions, sales builds another, and neither ends up being aligned with the actual product experience. These breaks in continuity cause buyers to experience fear, uncertainty, and doubt. Fear that they are making a mistake. Uncertainty about the essential nature of the company. And doubt that the company offers the best solution.

In the next chapter, I will describe how to define the quality of the experience your company wants to create. All I'm trying to establish for now is that in order to shape customer perceptions pursuant to creating vendor preference, we must clearly define the quality of experience we are trying to create and we must deliver it consistently across moments in brand, marketing, sales, product, and customer success.

Beyond Blocking and Tackling

Before we move on, there's still a question that must be answered: How does customer experience design directly address the steady decline of performance in the blocking and tackling era? In other words, why is customer experience the solution rather than a distraction?

Over the course of the last 20 years or so, blocking and tackling has come to define our strategies in sales and marketing rather than enabling them. A primary unintended consequence of the Software-as-a-Service transformation was go-to-market process assimilation across the entire tech industry. Everyone ended up running the same playbook based on a linear customer journey. This core process assimilation repositioned the axis of competitive advantage. Brand, marketing, and sales became more about playing the same game better rather than changing the game. In turn, performance optimization became the primary source of outperformance.

Performance optimization in this context drove companies to increasingly focus on the low-probability outcomes of metrics-based conversion rather than the high-probability outcomes of experience. In other words, it became much more important to drive one lead from 100 marketing contacts than to create a compelling experience for all 100 people—more important to close one out of five proposals than to become the preferred vendor for all five accounts. As the playing field became more crowded, the relentless focus on low-probability outcomes resulted in strategies that increasingly created the *worst* experiences for the *most* number of people. More to the point, metrics-based performance goals in marketing and sales became the strategy, instead of ways to measure whether the real strategy was producing the desired business outcomes. And this has most often led to initiatives in sales and marketing that temporarily boost performance in one area, but harm performance in other areas. Here is an (all-too-common) example.

A learning management software company has a marketing qualified lead (MQL) goal for marketing. The company has many themes and campaign groups for display ads, but ads derived from the phrase *employee engagement* perform better than ads derived from the phrase *learning outcomes*. To optimize performance against marketing goals (MQLs), marketing shifts more money into the *employee engagement* ad group and away from the *learning outcomes* ad group. At the same time, the cost of *employee engagement* ads keeps going up because the number of companies buying the related search phrases is increasing faster than relevant search volume. In the short run, the marketing team is able to hit their MQL goals, but over time, costs will continue to increase and results will continue to decrease. Meanwhile, sales is very proficient at talking about *learning outcomes* but not so much when it comes to *employee engagement*; and so, as *employee engagement* leads go up and *learning outcomes* leads go down (not because of market trends, but because of ad spend decisions), the sales team's ability to convert MQLs to sales qualified leads (SQLs) is negatively impacted.

As conversion rates go down in sales, sales management seeks to optimize performance in MQL-to-SQL conversion, starting with win-loss analysis. Research data indicates that many prospects are most interested in *employee engagement* and disappointed in the company's solution from this perspective. Sales zeroes in on the "spike" in interest in *employee engagement* and their poor sales conversion performance against that theme. Not knowing this spike was caused directly by an ad portfolio decision (and associated nurture streams) focused on the theme of *employee engagement*, sales mistakes this increase in interest for a market trend. Responding to these insights from the win-loss analysis, they conduct sales training and create multiple sales enablement tools focused on the theme of *employee engagement*. They rewrite their SDR outreach cadences. They make significant changes to their sales-ready messaging. And they successfully increase conversion rates. But the problem continues to manifest downstream.

Let's fast-forward to the product experience, where a significant number of new customers have now been convinced that the company's learning management solution is a great solution for *employee engagement*. These customers are disappointed to find that the product and customer success experiences have very little to do with *employee engagement* and a whole lot to do with *learning outcomes*. Whether the hardcore focus on *learning outcomes* helps or hurts *employee engagement* is a constant source of debate between customer success and customers. But what becomes absolutely clear to customers within a few months of using the product is that the essential nature and defining characteristics of the company and product are anchored in *outcomes*, not *engagement*. And so this subgroup of new customers starts a trend of declining customer satisfaction and increased churn.

Product and customer success respond to the negative trends and the feedback of dissatisfied customers by adding *employee engagement* features—maybe even an entire product. And within 18 months, the whole damn company is a hot mess, caught between two different groups of customers with radically different interests. One group is focused on *learning outcomes* and is dismayed by what feels like the company's shifting focus. And the other group is focused on *employee engagement*, dissatisfied from the start and pressing the company to catch up with their strategic orientation.

In this very familiar example, it should be clear how performance optimizations based on the metrics-based goals of our prevailing blocking and tackling led to one bad decision after another in each domain of the company.

But how would a holistic approach to customer experience design have helped?

The Power of Holistic Customer Experience

For starters, a holistic customer experience vision—a clear definition of the quality of experience the company wanted to create across all moments—could have established that the company's essential nature and defining characteristics are rooted in *outcomes*, not *engagement*. At the very least, this would have caused marketing to critically evaluate whether a marketing thread focused on *employee engagement* was reinforcing or eroding the overall perceptions of the company, brand, and product it wishes to establish. Second, customer experience design would have focused the company on delivering a consistent quality of moments across the entire customer experience instead of optimizing against the myopic, metrics-based goals of a single domain. This may have prevented sales from changing their message to something they perceived customers wanted to hear instead of resting confidently in what *they* wanted *customers* to hear. Finally, a customer experience perspective would have considered the much broader issue of the experience being created for the vast majority of people who do not become MQLs or SQLs. This would result in decisions that bring sales and marketing campaigns into greater alignment with the desired customer experience rather than decisions to change the experience for everyone in an effort to optimize short-run performance based only on the perceptions of the very few who are currently engaged in the sales experience.

Companies that are able to orient around a definitive customer experience vision, strategy, and design multiply the go-to-market impact of everything they do. When every moment (such as a marketing campaign) is designed based on the immutable quality of the perception the company is trying to achieve, and when there is continuity between all moments, every investment has an impact on current goal attainment and *future purchase intent creation*. Companies that build high levels of engagement prior to the development or creation of purchase intent find that the pressure to manufacture leads and sales opportunities in short time frames is significantly reduced. And that makes it much less likely that you will create moments that successfully drive short-run outcomes but mortgage future outcomes because of breaks in continuity.

As I mentioned earlier, I am presenting a holistic model that emphasizes the importance of the whole (the customer experience) and the interdependence of all of its parts (brand, marketing, sales, product, and customer success). Accordingly, everyone in the company has a responsibility to be true to the customer experience. And not just in the context of the small number of customers who make it from conversion point to conversion point in that part of the buyer's journey that their department is responsible for. But to everyone who interacts with the company, and especially the vast majority who don't become customers today, but may consider becoming customers at some point in the future. The specific strategies utilized to shape the customer experience may differ from domain to domain within a company, but everyone has a critical role to play in shaping perceptions to develop vendor preference now and in the future. And that role, specifically, is to *deliver* the customer experience.

But what is being delivered exactly? Great question …

CHAPTER 8

Experience Vision

Experience Vision: The (1) essential nature and (2) defining characteristics of the customer experience a company wishes to create.

We now have a clear definition of customer experience. And we have established our motivation—to shape customer perceptions of the quality of time spent with our company. And we understand that shaping these perceptions with intention is the most direct path to building vendor preference. But what are we doing again?

Let's get down to business. If you want to shape customer perceptions by designing and delivering a customer experience that establishes advantage over competitors, you must clearly define the (1) essential nature and (2) defining characteristics, or the *quality,* of the experience you wish to create. For an example, I'll turn to the customer experience design process for my own company, The Starr Conspiracy.

Essential Nature

When we embarked on the quest to capture our experience vision, we started by reviewing the other existential concepts we had wrestled with over the years like purpose, vision, and values. Our *purpose* at The

Starr Conspiracy is to create abundance. But the notion of abundance also shows up in our *vision* and *values* and every other aspirational concept we've ever pursued. That's because the quest for abundance is a constant in what is otherwise, by design, an inherently chaotic company. For us, abundance does not mean making everyone rich; it means living rich lives by developing an abundance mindset. That may sound flaky to you, but it's a real thing to us. More on abundance later.

When it came time to define the essential nature of the customer experience we try to create, it was obvious that our experience vision was related to these other constructs in some significant way. I guess you could say we saw our experience vision as the applied version of our purpose. How do we create abundance? By sharing moments of abundance with others. So we defined "abundant experiences" as the essential nature of our desired customer experience.

Now, in an epic of tangents, I want to take us on another. Concepts like purpose, vision, mission, values, brand attributes, and many others are all trying to achieve similar outcomes but in different contexts. They all seek to articulate the existential aspirations of an organization. We want to create a vision or purpose that is more meaningful than simply earning a profit or growing really fast or whatever because we all have an innate desire to elevate the meaning and significance of our daily work, which is often quite mundane. But the purpose and vision are always related to the context of business performance. We create values because we want to give shape to the experience we're trying to create for ourselves and others. And we do it so that we can send subtle cues about how to behave—about the vibe we're trying to cultivate. But values are always related to the context of employee success.

So many existential constructs have emerged over time that they often end up bumping into each other. *Is that our mission or our purpose or our vision?* The reason they all bump into each other is because they are all trying to provide answers to the same fundamental questions: "What kind of people do we want to be? How do we want others to perceive us? How do we want to make others feel?" In other words, these existential concepts are all trying to define our *essential nature* within a specific context (e.g., business performance, employee success, etc.).

The experience vision is a higher-level existential concept because it does not try to contextualize this search for meaning. It simply seeks to answer the big questions directly. *What kind of people do we want to be? How do we want others to perceive us? How do we want to make others feel? **What is our essential nature?*** And because the experience vision is unapologetically existential in nature, and because it is not focused on a contextualized outcome but rather seeks to describe the experience we hope to create for ourselves and everyone else (across multiple contexts), it creates the foundation for more than just the customer experience—it also establishes the quality of the experience we aspire to create for employees and shareholders. And although I have written extensively about employee experience and shareholder experience elsewhere (and their relationship to customer experience), such a discussion is way beyond the scope of this book. And I would *really* like to keep writing about it here! But I'm afraid it would distract from my primary purpose.

In short (and because I can't help myself), the employee, customer, and shareholder experiences must all flow from a shared experience vision. You can't promise one thing to customers and something different to employees and shareholders; that's a formula for disaster. Let's say you are a health and wellness company that promises customers greater holistic well-being, but your own work environment is a dumpster fire of stress and strain. The gap between your employee experience and customer experience will be exacerbated by the observable disparity between the two realms of experience. And, eventually (probably gradually and then suddenly), the negative employee experience will wreak havoc on both the customer experience and the shareholder experience.

In our own example, we found that the essential nature of our experience vision was showing up all over the place—in our purpose, our vision, our values, and more. This could have been a source of frustration or confusion as we worked to spell out our experience vision. But we actually found the overlap reassuring. In our estimation, every time we asked ourselves existential questions that touched on our essential nature as people and as a company, we always came back to the same source—abundance. So the essential nature of our experience vision was hiding in plain sight.

When creating your company's experience vision, you may find that it's already showing up in these other existential concepts. These are great places to borrow from. Or you may find that previous attempts to capture the existential nature of things failed to produce something that feels authentic and durable. And so you might go through a process to create something entirely new. Both scenarios are okay. You should neither feel the need to create something entirely new nor to artificially extract the experience vision from other pre-existing existential concepts. You should only feel compelled to get to the bottom of the essential nature of your organization (which reveals itself in defining moments).

Now, in truth, there are many additional questions that may be used to assist with the discovery of your own authentic and unique experience vision. Questions about the kind of experience your customers value. Questions about the kind of experience created by your competitors. Questions about the quality of experience you currently provide. And even questions about the kind of experience you want to avoid. But that's yet another tangent and I'll spare you.

In The Starr Conspiracy example, we agreed that the essential nature of our experience vision is "abundant experiences." But there was still work to be done in order to make the experience vision actionable. We still needed to articulate the defining characteristics.

Defining Characteristics

What is an *abundant* customer experience exactly? Our purpose (to create abundance) was derived from my personal belief in, and aspiration to, live in an abundance mindset (as opposed to a scarcity mindset). The hallmarks of an abundance mindset include recognizing the power of one's own thoughts and vision, practicing gratitude, seeing plenty instead of lack, thinking big, focusing on opportunities rather than problems, emphasizing what's working rather than what's broken, sharing freely, cultivating mastery, being a learn-it-all instead of a know-it-all, embracing change, practicing situational awareness, developing an internal locus of control, and more.

That's an awful lot and, to be honest, some of these aspects of abundance appeal more to us than others. So we selected four defining characteristics of abundance that we feel most compelled to deliver:

- Think big
- Share freely
- Focus on opportunities
- Practice gratitude

With all of the above in mind, our customer experience vision can be clearly articulated in the following *customer experience vision statement:*

The Starr Conspiracy creates abundant customer experiences by thinking big, sharing freely, focusing on opportunities, and practicing gratitude.

So back to the main idea here. As we work to shape customer perceptions by actually delivering on our customer experience vision in everything we do (as opposed to simply promising it), we are left with some simple guiding principles to steer our strategies across the entire company. *In everything we do, we must create abundant customer experiences.* And the test for whether we're creating abundant experiences is simple:

1. Are we thinking big?
2. Are we sharing freely?
3. Are we focusing on opportunities?

4. Are we practicing gratitude?

Applying the Experience Vision

I'll describe the entire customer experience framework in the next chapter, but for now let's take it down a level and observe how our experience vision translates into strategy and tactics within a few of the different domains of our own customer experience. I'll use the marketing, sales, and product experiences to provide quick examples.

Our *experience goal* in marketing at The Starr Conspiracy is to create abundant customer experiences. So we design marketing campaigns that go beyond simply promising abundance (as soon as you become a client). Rather, we design marketing campaigns that actually deliver abundance. And what are the defining characteristics of an abundant experience?

- **We bring big ideas to the table,** both in terms of the ideas we share in a campaign and the ideas that guide our campaign design.

- **We share our insights generously.** For example, our renowned Work Tech Weekly newsletter (written by Steve Smith of The Starr Conspiracy) provides an abundance of high-quality insights about the Work Tech industry that other firms would keep behind a paywall—and we don't even make you fill out a form to read it.

- **We focus on opportunities** rather than constantly lamenting all the things that are broken in the world. *Now it's true that this book is based on a big problem in sales and marketing, but having an abundance mindset does not mean ignoring big problems—it means bringing big ideas to the table and identifying opportunities presented by change and disruption.* And we practice gratitude by reminding people of the good stuff, presenting big opportunities, and constantly reflecting on all the things we're grateful for.

- **And we never miss a chance to say thank you.**

The same is true for our sales experience. Our salespeople don't promise abundance down the road. They deliver it at every moment of the sales experience. By bringing big ideas to sales conversations. By sharing time and resources freely. By focusing on the prospective customer's opportunities rather than creating a false sense of fear about all the problems they're experiencing. And by demonstrating our gratitude for the time they share with us and the things they teach us along the way. Perhaps there is no better example of an abundant defining moment in our sales experience than our business planning sessions. In these sessions, we spend as much as an entire day with a prospective customer and focus on white-boarding solutions for their company. We don't charge anything for our time or travel, and we don't hold anything back.

And when it comes to our product experience—the experience we create for our active clients? Let's just say the abundance flows freely. We are constantly on the hunt for big ideas that change our clients' destinies, whether those ideas are related to the project we're working on or not. We share our expertise freely; we've never been accused of "nickeling and diming" our clients to death or withholding insights and recommendations simply because we're waiting for the right opportunity to pitch them on a new project. And we never forget to demonstrate our gratitude for the trust they have placed in us.

I'm about to start writing about the customer experience framework now. But before I do, I want to recap where we are and foreshadow what comes after our discussion of The Starr Conspiracy customer experience framework. (Is it still foreshadowing if you say you're doing it? A ghostwriter would have caught that!)

At this point, we have:

- Established that blocking and tackling alone is no longer sufficient to create competitive advantage, and that ...

- Sales and marketing performance is in decline because we're all doing the same things

- Presented a holistic customer experience as the solution
- Defined customer experience as the perception of the quality of time spent with a company
- Discussed the need for shaping perceptions to create vendor preference in the minds of customers
- Explored the process of creating an experience vision
- Emphasized the difference between delivering on the customer experience and only promising it
- Distinguished between the essential nature and defining characteristics of an experience vision
- Provided a few light examples of how The Starr Conspiracy delivers on our customer experience in marketing, sales, and product

Now I'm going to describe my simple framework for customer experience. But I want to make a point first (foreshadowing!): Most performance issues are caused by breaks in continuity between domains of the customer experience. When continuity of experience is not maintained across brand, marketing, sales, product, and customer success, bad shit happens. Most of the time, when companies have a performance issue in sales or marketing, they think the issue is isolated to that specific domain of the customer experience. But often, upon closer inspection, it becomes obvious that the performance issue is actually caused by conflicting qualities of experience *between* different domains. That's the holistic part of customer experience— it's as much (or more) about how the interdependent components of customer experience work together than it is about blocking and tackling excellence in each component. I have a story to tell about that. But first, let's dive into the framework.

CHAPTER 9

The Starr Conspiracy Customer Experience Framework

The Starr Conspiracy customer experience framework has three components: experience vision, the five domains of customer experience, and defining moments.

What good is knowing the benefits of delivering a consistent customer experience without knowing exactly how to create one? So here's exactly how to do it. And more importantly, how to create a unique customer experience that is authentic to the essential nature and defining characteristics of your company. And even more importantly, how to create a unique customer experience that drives your competitive advantage, improves performance across the company, fixes persistent issues that were previously thought to be unfixable, and unlocks new opportunities for innovation and leadership. That's a tall order! But I think we can get there. So here we go.

But first, what is a framework? (Lol.) A true framework is nothing more than a simple conceptual structure that communicates the components of an approach. It's not a blueprint with detailed instructions for how to completely build the thing out. But it's a great way to gain a better understanding of what should be built, and it helps people visualize the process they will need to go through to implement the concept. In the end, the final product might look very different for each person or company who uses the same framework. But the hallmarks of the framework should be evident in each implementation. That's what this is—a simple conceptual structure that communicates the fundamental components of customer experience.

I argue that this framework is, in and of itself, an innovation. As far as I am aware, there exists no other framework that articulates the primary components of customer experience in such a manner and with such detail. (And, to be clear, it's not for lack of research. I've spent the last three years researching, developing, and testing this framework.) And since I have laid claim to a much broader interpretation of the concept of customer experience, it stands to reason that there are no equivalent frameworks out there.

To be clear, there are tons of other bodies of work about customer experience, but most of them are limited in scope and do not delve into the subject with as much depth and detail as what is found here. And most importantly, most of what exists out there is not backed up by actual field work. You might find analyst reports here and there outlining some basic concepts in product experience or customer success. Or you might find some vendor white papers that position customer experience as a system of metrics, KPIs, and analytics that seek to provide insight into the performance of your current customer experience (e.g., customer satisfaction, customer effort score, Net Promoter Score®, customer churn and retention, first response time, average resolution time, customer lifetime value, etc.), but such sources are once again limited in scope and also fail to describe the process of designing and implementing an intentional customer experience that results in these measurable outcomes *while also differentiating from competitors*. In the worst case scenario, these metrics-only interpretations of customer experience lead to metrics-based blocking and tackling initiatives that result in breaks in experience continuity.

In sharp contrast, this framework redefines customer experience as much broader and intrinsically holistic in nature with implications for every person and function within a tech company. And it provides components for actually designing and implementing a differentiated customer experience. And perhaps the most innovative part of this framework is that it's simple. One of the shared traits of my actionable frameworks over the decades is their ability to render potentially complex concepts in very simple terms. A good framework is one that is easy to understand and engage with, but that immediately yields deep insights and new, productive paths forward. I believe this framework achieves these goals.

The Starr Conspiracy customer experience framework has three components:

1. The quality (essential nature and defining characteristics) of your desired customer experience must be captured in an **experience vision.**

2. Your experience vision must become a shared dimension of strategy in each of the **five domains of customer experience**: (1) brand experience, (2) marketing experience, (3) sales experience, (4) product experience, and (5) customer success.

3. To achieve the desired quality of experience in each domain, you must identify and elevate the **defining moments** of the experience in that domain.

Okay. That's it. Now let's tear it apart.

CHAPTER 10

Revisiting Experience Vision

The quality (essential nature and defining characteristics) of your desired customer experience must be delineated in an experience vision.

We have already discussed the why and the how of experience vision. But a few points are worth revisiting in this new context of The Starr Conspiracy customer experience framework. First, the experience vision is absolutely essential to the success of your customer experience strategy—it is the part of the framework that provides the material for a holistic customer experience. It's simply not enough to drive for a "good" or "better" customer experience as defined by metrics and KPIs like customer satisfaction, NPS, and customer retention. Without a unifying experience vision, individual domains of customer experience may strive for domain-level blocking and tackling excellence only to find that excellent performance in some domains is masking sharp breaks in experience continuity that manifest as problems in other domains. Unfortunately, these problems are often hard to trace back to the actual source.

We'll talk more about this later on, but a common example is found in many tech companies where the marketing experience appears to be performing well (consistently hitting all the lead goals) and the product experience appears to be performing well (based on lagging customer satisfaction metrics), but sales begins struggling to hit goals. This usually results in a teardown of the sales function. But when evaluated through the lens of holistic customer experience, it frequently becomes apparent that marketing is driving leads with messages, positions, or keyword strategies that are not representative of the actual product experience. For example, if a company has a really amazing talent acquisition solution but marketing is promoting a campaign theme based on employee performance (because the concepts are indirectly related and the campaign group performs well), it's highly likely that prospective customers attracted by this ad group will have an expectation for the product that is not aligned with the product's strengths. And the more successful this campaign group is, the more it gets promoted (because it really helps marketing hit their MQL goals), leading to a higher share of inbound leads with an employee performance expectation.

In this scenario, sales gets caught in the middle. The blocking and tackling of the sales experience is probably fine, but when certain prospective customers entering the sales experience have formed their perceptions based on a thread of marketing campaigns promoting a position that is successful at driving leads but not completely aligned with the actual product experience, these prospective customers bounce off the demo (as soon as they get a look at the product). Or worse, they become dissatisfied new customers down the road. Again, it's not that the product is deficient (the lagging customer satisfaction metrics prove it). It's just that these particular prospective customers formed a different perception of the product experience and the break in continuity was jarring enough to sow fear, uncertainty, and doubt. It resulted in a loss of trust. Thus the company ends up working hard to solve the wrong problem and inadvertently breaks some things that were actually working just fine.

Second, the experience vision must serve to integrate the strategies across all domains. Over the years, we've all witnessed the negative impacts caused by shifting strategic leadership from one domain to the next. Some companies over-rotate to a product-led strategy.

Others over-rotate to a sales- or marketing-led strategy. But all of these strategic orientations miss the point. Strategy should flow from a unified vision for the customer experience that a company strives to create, resulting in clear mandates for each domain that allow for decentralized pursuits of excellent domain-level performance but that always reinforce the experiences created in other domains (with minimal coordination) rather than contradicting, shifting, resetting, or diminishing them. Marketing shouldn't lead product. And product shouldn't lead marketing. Both should be led by the customer experience vision.

Finally, your experience vision must be unique and authentic to your company. This vision is instrumental to the essential nature and defining characteristics of your resulting customer experience. No, it's more than instrumental. It is the one thing. So if the experience you end up creating does not differentiate you from competitors in obvious ways, you will not find the competitive advantage you seek. Even if your "customer experience metrics" are lights-out good.

CHAPTER 11

The Five Domains of Customer Experience

Your experience vision must become a shared dimension of strategy in each of the five domains of customer experience: (1) brand experience, (2) marketing experience, (3) sales experience, (4) product experience, and (5) customer success.

There are several important innovations and opportunities to unpack here, so let's get to it.

First of all, it's a significant mindshift to expand the notion of customer experience to include all of these functional areas. On the one hand, it's fairly intuitive to acknowledge that brand, marketing, and sales are related to product and customer experience. But it's quite another to commit to a holistic model for customer experience that directly links performance across functional areas. And doing so often results in counterintuitive strategies for brand, marketing, and sales. For example, it's hard to imagine a context in which pulling back on aggressive efforts to set appointments and book demos makes sense for sales. But when viewed through the lens of holistic customer experience, it's *sometimes* the case that metrics-driven efforts to convert MQLs to sales opportunities break the continuity of your desired customer experience for the vast majority of prospective customers, resulting in diminished opportunity and growth over time. It's especially hard to draw this conclusion when sales *appears to be* hitting goals!

Second, there is a significant innovation that often goes unnoticed here. That is the clear distinction between brand experience and marketing experience. Brand and marketing experiences are not an either/or model decision. In other words, companies do not decide whether they are going to create a brand experience *or* a marketing experience. Both experiences exist in nature and they are both critical to the overall customer experience. Just because you don't acknowledge your brand experience does not mean you don't have one. It just means that you aren't in control of it. And that can have catastrophic consequences. Later I'll provide some specific details about the unique characteristics and strategic goals for each domain (including an entire chapter dedicated to brand). But for now, it's sufficient to acknowledge that none of the domains in this framework are contrived. They simply exist as unique domains of the overall customer experience and are processed by customers in unique ways.

Third, I want to dispel the notion that customer experience is a linear process. It's just not. Customer experience is not a journey that starts with brand and ends with customer success. It's not a funnel or pipeline. It's not a numbers game (though numbers are obviously descriptive and assist in performance management). Customer experience is non-sequential and chaotic, and the journey is more like jumping on and off a merry-go-round than going down a slide. People get on and off in different places all the time. But the overall perception of their customer experience is stitched together from all the different moments in different domains. Therefore, a company should not optimize its customer experience around a linear journey. Rather, it should optimize around the defining moments created in each domain, ensuring that all moments are designed based on the unifying experience vision.

Let me give you an example. Somewhere today, someone is

starting a new job where they will be expected to learn and use your product. This will be their first exposure to your company. They were not familiar with your brand, they never received any of your marketing, and they didn't participate in the sales experience. So their entire perception of the quality of time spent with your company will be mostly formed by the defining moments of the product and customer success experiences.

Let's say that six months from now, this same person is promoted and encouraged to attend a major trade show like the HR Technology® Conference & Exhibition (HR Tech). While there, maybe they meet some people from another company who are evaluating your product. These other people have experienced many brand, marketing, and sales moments. But they haven't seen a demo, engaged with the product experience, or worked through an issue with customer success. What happens when everyone compares notes? Will the overall experience for all parties be reinforced or diminished? And what impact will that have on the current customer and the prospective customers?

And what happens 18 months from now when our person accepts a position with a new company and is put in charge of evaluating and implementing a new product like yours? They got off the merry-go-round in one place and got back on somewhere else. If what they experience in brand, marketing, and sales is radically different from their previous product and customer success experiences, will that be okay? Or will the break in continuity create just enough fear, uncertainty, and doubt that they will open their product evaluation to other vendors. And might that lead to a shift in the early preferred vendor status? Maybe to a competitor who is promising more than you in their marketing and sales experience (and it sure sounds good compared with the product experience they've been having with you). And since they are unencumbered by an actual product experience with the competitor, who are they more likely to believe? You—the company that promises things in marketing and sales that don't line up with the actual product experience? Or the competitor that hasn't had to live up to their promises yet?

The only way to control for the chaotic nature of real customer experiences is to optimize around the consistency of defining moments in each domain. In real life, we don't get the benefit of controlling the sequence of the journey itself. Therefore, we must control the quality and consistency of defining moments across the customer experience.

CHAPTER 12

On Brand

Great brand experience design conveys brand power to all other domains of customer experience. When excellent brand work is lined up with excellent brand strategy and both are used to create excellent brand experiences, the primary assets of brand (like visual design and brand message) convey brand power in all other domains and contexts.

There is no topic in marketing more controversial than brand. So, sure. I'll weigh in.

Most disagreements about brand are rooted in definitions. Like many of the concepts in this book, brand means many different things to many different people. Some people are obsessed with noun versions. Other people are obsessed with verb versions. I am obsessed with redefining brand, and that sometimes confuses people. To muddy the waters even more, I present brand here as one domain of customer experience. But many believe that brand is the base of the pyramid, the center of the wheel, or whatever other metaphor you want to use to describe a world where brand is the source of everything else. To clarify my own position about brand, I'm going to cut it up into a million little pieces.

I want to start by talking about models and illustrations. Everyone wants a picture to describe concepts that can otherwise seem complex.

But often, in the search for the right illustration, the true meaning of the model can be lost. That's why I have made the intentional decision to avoid illustrating The Starr Conspiracy customer experience framework. For one thing, pretty pictures are one of the big reasons we're in this mess to begin with. Pipelines and funnels and buyer's journeys all look great when they're drawn from left to right or top to bottom. But in this book I hope to establish that the customer experience is non-sequential and chaotic. You can't control the order of experiences—you can only control the quality and consistency of moments throughout the customer experience. For another thing, the true power of my customer experience framework would be lost if it were reduced to a sequential, linear model. And there are several reasons why. First, every domain of customer experience impacts every other domain. The work in the brand domain, for instance, is not limited to the brand domain. Brand work happens in every domain. The work in the product domain is not limited to the product domain. There is product work to be done in every domain. If I were to put *all things brand* in a brand box, it would seem to imply that brand work is only done for brand campaigns, or only to drive direct brand results. And that's simply not true. Brand work happens in all domains and lifts marketing, sales, product, and customer success results as much as direct brand results.

Second, nearly any kind of illustration would imply an order of things. Does the customer experience start with brand experience and end with customer success? No. It can start anywhere and end anywhere and bounce around between domains for infinity. Imagine a pinball machine where the customer is the ball and the vendor is the board. What about the flippers? *Those are just the hands of chaos, man.*

Finally, illustrations are mostly process maps and flowcharts in disguise. Customer experience is not a flowchart. It's more like a chaos pendulum. The unique motion of a single customer experience appears random, just like the unique motion of a single swing of a chaos pendulum. We don't have enough information to predict the sequence of moments in a single customer experience. But it's actually not random at all. It's chaotic. If we view all customer experiences in aggregate, we're still not able to predict the specific motion of a single customer experience, but we are able to gain insight into the moments that are most frequently shared between different customer experiences (even if they don't happen in the same order).

Our job is not to predict or control the sequence. It's neither our job to predict where the chaos pendulum is going to be next, nor to force the pendulum into a predictable motion. Just like it's not our job to predict the next moment in a customer experience or to force customers into a flowchart. It's our job to control the quality of the moments the customer passes through, knowing that, over time, most customer experiences will pass through the same moments (though rarely in the same order). I'm probably going too deep into chaos theory now, so I'll spare you. But it's worth noting that our prevailing blocking and tackling in sales and marketing mistakes chaos for randomness and views deviation from our desired sequence of events as lack of engagement. Thus, the vast majority of customers who do not follow our prescribed buyer's journey (read: flowchart) are dismissed as unqualified, detractors, or a waste of our time. Just to say it out loud, that's not good.

What Is Brand?

Back to the point. Brand is not the beginning or end of anything. And it's not the source from which all other strategies flow. It simply *is*. Now, all that being said, one of the benefits of classifying brand as a single domain in customer experience is to give shape to the work that must be done to create brand experiences and to convey brand power to moments in other domains. There are certain talents required to create brand experiences, and those are mostly on the creative side. And those talents must be honed through the acquisition of brand-specific skills. Simply being creative doesn't make one effective at creating brand experiences. That creativity must be enriched with domain knowledge and skills. And that's why it is beneficial to group certain types of work and strategy in a brand domain. Otherwise, the brand part of everything ends up being distributed to people and departments who often don't understand brand strategy and don't spend every day learning how to activate it. That point aside, brand experience is simply different from marketing experience because it is processed by customers in a different way.

So what is brand? I'm going to embrace the chaos by saying that brand is many things. But, for the purpose of implementing this customer experience framework, it's useful to distinguish between several different, valid meanings of brand. Here, I'll focus on three aspects of brand: brand experience, brand strategy, and brand work. But I'm going to describe them in reverse order, starting with the subatomic particles and building up to the atoms and molecules. So let's start with brand work.

There is really no way to talk about brand work without oversimplifying it. So I'll start by saying that brand work is art and writing. Those are the talent parts. You can teach good writing, but you can't teach great writing. You can teach good art, but you can't teach great art. The best brand people in the world are undeniable talents. But brand work must also be bolstered by skills involving strategy and execution. The greatest artists and writers in the world often make terrible brand marketers. Not because of their talent, but because of their lack of brand-specific knowledge and skills. In short, don't underestimate the talent or the skills; both are necessary. There are fundamental, blocking and tackling components of brand work that create the infrastructure for the brand experience, but it's the level of talent and skill that provides a true advantage in brand experience.

The two most important components of brand work are the visual identity (art) and brand message (writing). The blocking and tackling is important here, but it's not enough. A blocking and tackling approach to visual identity will give you a solid-but-forgettable logo, color palette, and visual design system. And a blocking and tackling approach to message will give you a serviceable (but cookie-cutter) "unique value proposition." And, y'all, I love me some Geoffrey Moore, but *Crossing the Chasm* was written more than 30 years ago. And Moore was writing during the heyday of the blocking and tackling era. His work changed my life. But it's time to move on. Brand work has to be elevated to the level of brand strategy and brand experience in this new era of customer experience.

Brand strategy is the combination of brand goals and brand work, placed within the context of specific business goals. Business goals can vary significantly between companies, but brand goals are relatively consistent and straightforward. The three primary *brand goals* of brand strategy are:

- Brand recognition
- Functional association
- Brand attributes

There are very few business goals that don't require high levels of performance from the three primary brand goals. Whether you're seeking to grow revenue or profit, or even achieve an end-game outcome like an acquisition by a strategic buyer, brand goals multiply the results of business goals. Maybe if your business goal was to wind down operations, brand goals would be less important. But I can make the opposite case.

Brand recognition is a more specific way to describe *brand awareness.* Do people even know that you exist? That's brand recognition. During the last few decades or so, I have studied the relationship between brand recognition and business results. Through my research, I have identified two areas where I believe brand recognition *causes* business results. But if you're familiar with the academic headache of proving causation versus correlation, you'll understand why I don't make that definitive claim here. There is enough junk science in the world of business; I don't want to add to it.

But I know for a fact that brand recognition is correlated with market share *and* conversion rates. I conducted two major studies starting in 2010 and I have confirmed the same findings in subsequent studies for more than a decade now. First, I launched a study of the relationship between brand recognition and market share for a cohort of Human Capital Management (HCM) firms built around Ultimate Software (now UKG). In the study, I measured open-market brand recognition and correlated those results with market share. The data was definitive. Brand recognition precedes market share order. In other words, if I rank companies from one to 10 based on their brand recognition, that ranking will be reflected in market share order about 12 to 18 months later. The lesson here is simple. If you want to increase market share, you have to increase brand recognition against competitors first.

The second study measured brand recognition against marketing and sales response and conversion rates for a cohort of talent management companies built around Taleo (acquired by Oracle in 2012). Again, the results were definitive (and have remained so in similar studies). When similar direct marketing campaigns for competing companies are sent to the same media list, the response rates correlate with brand recognition within that media audience. In other words, if I send the same marketing campaign for 10 learning management companies to the *Chief Learning Officer* email list, the response rates would be highest for the company with the most brand recognition within that audience and lowest for the company with the least. And everything in between would correlate as well. Another simple lesson—if you want to increase your response and conversion rates, increase your brand recognition within the communities you're marketing to. As Dr. Seuss writes, "To the world, you may be one person; but to one person, you may be the world."

It was this simple lesson that led to The Starr Conspiracy's creation of the "takeover campaign" model. Knowing that only the largest tech companies have the budget to impact brand recognition across the entire industry, we created a strategy for paid industry media that focuses first on increasing brand recognition within chosen media communities, and then transitions from brand marketing to direct marketing as brand recognition increases. We *take over* the media community, establishing a dominant share of voice before cashing in via higher response rates later.

While brand recognition provides insight into how aware people are of your company's existence, functional association provides insight into whether people know what your company does. For example, nearly everyone has heard of Workday. But how many people are aware that Workday offers payroll, financial management, talent management, workforce management, vendor management, employee engagement measurement, and more? Strong functional association has a direct impact on revenue and market share. This is especially true when functions change, such as after a merger or acquisition, or with the launch of a new product line. The worst time for someone to find out that you offer a solution they need is right after they have bought it from someone else! Often, I work with companies that are shocked to learn how little even their current customers know about their total solution portfolio, much less prospective customers. Fortunately, as far as brand problems go, functional association is easily fixed. But you don't fix functional association by focusing only on the brand experience. Functional association (like everything else) is a thread that must be pulled through the brand, marketing, sales, product, and customer success experiences.

Finally, the third component of brand strategy is brand attributes. If brand recognition is *who you are* and functional association is *what you do*, then brand attributes are *what you're like.* Of the three components of brand strategy, brand attributes offer the tiebreaker between competing vendors. Two different companies can have similar brand recognition and functional associations, but the decision by customers to choose one over the other will largely be based on their emotional perceptions of the companies. And these perceptions are formed in no small part by the brand attributes of a company.

Brand attributes should not be confused with the experience vision. Your experience vision speaks to the essential nature and defining characteristics of the *experience* you want to create. On the other hand, brand attributes speak to what you bring to the table in those experiences. For example, our experience vision at The Starr Conspiracy is to create abundant customer experiences. But our brand attributes are *smart, fun,* and *creative.* So we come to the *experience table* as smart, fun, and creative people ready to create an abundant experience. We don't try to create a smart experience or a fun experience or a creative experience. That's just going to happen because of who we are as people and a company. But we will harness those attributes to create an *abundant* experience. From this perspective, brand attributes speak to who we are as people and as a company, while the experience vision speaks to the quality of experience we want to create in shared moments with others.

There is an important relationship between brand work and brand strategy that is worth talking about. As I mentioned earlier, probably the two most important components of brand work are the visual identity and brand message. But how does the approach to these two components impact the performance of the brand strategy? Let's start with the visual identity. Based on the primary goals of brand strategy, the goal of the visual identity should be to activate brand recognition, functional associations, and brand attributes. If we make the simplifying assumption that your visual identity is composed of a logo, color palette, and visual design system (or visual language), how does this work impact the performance of your brand strategy?

Visual Identity

Let's use the logo as an example. *Like, what is a logo even for, man?* A logo is just a visual symbol. It's a picture that references something else. Specifically, it's a visual symbol that references the people, places, and things associated with your company. With regard to brand strategy, it's the most concentrated instrument for brand recognition and recall. When the logo is used in the context of something like a marketing campaign, it becomes a way to tag content and invest it with all the power of the brand in just 250 horizontal pixels. In this example, the content of the campaign takes on an added dimension because of the brand power associated with the logo. Take any thought leadership article. Now put an Accenture logo on it. The content just became more meaningful, right? But for you to get the same effect from your logo, people need to *recognize* it. And they need to *recall* what your company does and what your company is like.

You know how people say you have to see a logo seven times (or whatever) before you remember it? Well, that's bullshit. For people to remember a logo, *it has to be memorable.* Sure, being memorable can be a function of repetition. But the more inherently memorable a logo is, the fewer times people need to see it to recognize it. For all you budget hawks out there, that means you'll have to spend less money to get people to recognize your brand. A well-designed, unique logo is a more efficient tool for driving brand recognition and recall. And that's not just important in the context of recognizing your logo in a vacuum. It's also (incredibly) important in the context of transferring brand power to the people, places, or things associated with your company. See that person at the trade show in a red shirt? That's just some person in a red shirt. See that person at the trade show in a red Oracle shirt? That's an *Oracle* person.

So when it comes time to design a logo, you need to be aware that visual design is a powerful instrument for driving brand recognition and catalyzing recall of your functional associations and brand attributes. Obviously, the first objective is to design something memorable. That's just smart brand strategy. People remember pictures better than words, so the logo mark (the picture part) is where the action is. Take this opportunity to be bold. Make yourself nervous. Because if your design doesn't make you a little bit nervous, no one else is even going to notice. Here's a fun test. Show your logo to 10 people. Twenty-four hours later, ask them to sketch it from memory. Did anyone get close? If not, you're going to be spending a bunch of money to create recognition and recall. How much? The last time I measured brand recognition against marketing budgets in the Work Tech segment, the average cost per point of recognition was $2.1 million annually. That's sad—and it's unnecessary. It's also a direct reflection of the widespread rejection of high-quality brand strategy by most tech companies.

So I've covered the role of a well-designed *logo* in *brand recognition*. But the *logo* is only one asset in a visual identity. (In fact, in a world where everyone has a website, one could argue that the visual design system itself can make a greater impact than the logo.) And *brand recognition* is only one of three primary goals of brand strategy. I know I've said this several times about different topics, but I could write a whole other book about brand experience. There's just so much to it. But I want to pull us back to the theme, so I'm going to sharpen my prose a bit. Everything I said about logos is also true for color palettes, design systems, and other visual brand assets. Color and design choices must be memorable and unique from competitors. The more recognizable, differentiated design layers that exist in your visual brand, the more effective your brand strategy will be. And not just when it comes to recognition.

Effective visual brand design is critical to establishing functional associations and brand attributes, but for different reasons. The connection between brand attributes and visual design ought to be pretty clear. Different design choices can be evocative of our brand attributes. We can use line, shape, form, space, texture, tone, and color to communicate human nuance. And the more successful we are in doing so, the more effective our entire brand strategy will be.

Functional associations, on the other hand, are rarely imbued in the highest-level visual brand elements, such as a logo. You can and should design a recognizable logo. And you can and should design a logo that evokes your brand attributes. But while you *can* design a logo that communicates your functional identity, you really shouldn't. Functional associations change too frequently. It is not the primary role of great design to directly communicate the functions. The primary role of great design is to create the context for functions to be successfully associated with the brand. Functional associations are primarily delivered in writing rather than art. But when the functions are repeatedly presented in a memorable and consistent visual design context, the odds that those functions will be associated with your brand down the road when it really matters increase significantly.

Brand Message

Brand message is another key component of the brand experience. A good message, much like a good visual brand, multiplies recognition, functional association, and brand attributes. How? First, brand recognition isn't just about putting a message in front of someone. It's about getting someone to remember it. And especially when they don't have it in front of them! A well-written, effective, and efficient brand message will stick in people's minds and resurface in moments that are beneficial to the formation of a positive vendor perception. Many years ago, The Starr Conspiracy rebranded SumTotal, an enterprise learning company that went on to be acquired by Cornerstone OnDemand in 2022. In addition to a highly effective visual brand, we also created a brand message anchored by the statement, "Humans are not Capital." This was just the right kind of message for the time—one that popped into people's minds every time they were having a very non-human experience with their current talent management system. That message had a significant impact on brand recognition.

A strong brand message also effectively communicates the functions of your solution. But it does so in a way that emphasizes the *association* part of functional associations. That is to say that a powerful brand message doesn't just list the functions of your product; it communicates them in such a way as to make it absurd to imagine any other set of functions could achieve the same goal. It has to be absolutely obvious that the functions of your product represent almost a moral obligation to do things the right and only way.

Finally, brand attributes are the things that make your message a *brand* message. Most often, your brand attributes are not going to show up in what you say, but in how you say it. I always think of Mike

Carden, currently the founder and CEO of Joyous, when I write about message and brand attributes. When Mike was still running Sonar6 (the company he founded and then sold to Cornerstone OnDemand), he didn't need to tell the world that his company was irreverent. Their brand message was simply, "Performance reviews that don't suck." Everyone got the picture.

Brand Moments

So what is the relationship between your brand experience and your brand work and brand strategy? Brand experience is the perception of the quality of time spent with your brand, where the meaning of "quality" is *essential nature and defining characteristics*. Brand experience is where your work and your strategy come together in moments shared with customers to achieve your customer experience goals and to shape vendor perception. Brand experience represents a different and additional design process to brand work and brand strategy. To put a fine point on it, brand experience is composed of the significant moments that customers share with your brand. Brand moments.

But what is a brand moment? When we consider the entire sweep of customer experience, it's much easier to recognize and describe marketing, sales, product, and customer success moments. Here are a few examples:

- Marketing moment: a prospective customer receives an email from marketing
- Sales moment: a salesperson delivers a product demo
- Product moment: the first time a customer logs in
- Customer success moment: a customer success manager resolves a product issue for a customer

Brand moments, however, are a little different—which is precisely why they are so important! Unlike the other domains of customer experience, brand moments mostly occur in contexts where there is no expectation for a direct channel of communication between the customer and the company, or where the ability to control the moment at scale does not exist. Let's think about it in terms of a brand campaign. Brand campaigns are designed to achieve the goals of brand strategy. In other words, brand campaigns are designed to directly increase brand recognition, functional association, and brand attributes. If a campaign is designed to drive leads, it is not a brand campaign—it's a marketing campaign. So a true brand campaign is often delivered in channels where there is no direct line of communication back to the company (like television, radio, outdoor, or print media). In channels such as these, one can always provide a QR code, a link, a phone number, or whatever—but most of the time, brand ads that provide these options are missing the point. Brand advertising is not about driving leads. Can brand advertising be delivered via direct marketing channels such as email? Absolutely. Brand strategy can be achieved in all domains of the customer experience. But that which creates a brand moment is defined by the goals it seeks to achieve. As Forrest Gump might say, "Brand is as brand does." If the *primary* strategy of the moment is to build brand recognition, functional association, or brand attributes, then it is a brand moment.

And here's a full-circle conclusion for brand experience. Great brand experience design conveys brand power to all other domains of customer experience. When excellent brand work is lined up with excellent brand strategy and both are used to create excellent brand experiences, the primary assets of brand (like visual design and message) convey brand power in all other domains and contexts. A marketing campaign performs better when the visual brand and message make it abundantly clear who the campaign is coming from, what they do for a living, and what they are like. Sales performs better when their communications are invested with brand power. Products built on effective brand design achieve higher engagement. And customer success drives better satisfaction and retention when backed by a powerful brand experience.

CHAPTER 13

Defining Moments

A defining moment is a point in time in which the essential nature or character of the company is revealed or identified.

The final component of my framework for customer experience is the design of defining moments. A deep understanding of defining moments provides the magic that powers this framework, because it's the defining moments that provide us with the most opportunity to shape perceptions and achieve breakthrough performance—the kind of performance that elevates competitive advantage beyond what may be conveyed by effective and efficient blocking and tackling alone.

Let's start by establishing a definition of defining moments. Then we can discuss how to identify and create them while providing more context for why they're so important. *A defining moment is a point in time in which the essential nature or character of the company is revealed or identified.*

In other words, customer experiences may be composed of thousands of moments—but only a few of these moments stand out from the others and end up defining the essential nature and character (quality) of the experience. These are the moments we can and should take control of to shape perceptions of the customer experience at scale.

This ought to be an incredibly liberating notion! Many people are relieved to learn that it's not the goal to architect and monitor every moment of the customer experience. Not only is that not necessary, but approaching customer experience with that perspective often results in attempts to fix things that aren't broken and long lists of projects and initiatives that prevent the most important things from being done. These other moments are the domain of effective blocking and tackling! Sure, defining moments most directly produce customer experience, but the steady hum of less essential moments that work the way they're supposed to while largely going unnoticed reinforce the quality of customer experience. In fact, it's effective blocking and tackling that allows companies to cash in on the benefits of well-designed defining moments! More on that later when I detail how defining moments improve all aspects of brand, marketing, and sales performance. But for now, back to defining moments.

Perhaps a deeper explanation of defining moments would be beneficial. Any experience is composed of moments. But *defining moments* come to cement a person's perception of the essential nature and defining characteristics of an experience. Our brains are not wired to record every moment that composes an experience. But it is essential that we categorize and catalog the overall quality of our experiences. Why? Because this is how we utilize our past experiences to sharpen future decision-making.

The Trip of a Lifetime

I'll give you an example. One summer, I rented an RV and took my family on a six-week tour of America. Let's call it an RV *experience*. At the time, my daughter was eight years old and my son was five. I remember that RV experience as the trip of a lifetime. I even had a hardcover coffee table book made that captures our greatest moments from the trip. It's titled *Our Super Awesome RV Adventure* and the cover features a photo of the four of us standing in front of Cinderella

Castle at Disney World.

I frequently reflect upon that trip because it brings me so much joy. I'll admit that I've forgotten a lot about it (even in such a short period of time). But I'll always remember the big moments—the defining moments. Last weekend, someone asked me about our route and the places we had stopped along the way. I really struggled to remember most of the details. But I vividly remember these moments:

- **The beginning:** I remember the speech I gave at the farewell dinner with close family and friends who had joined us to mark the occasion of our departure. (Yes, I gave a speech. I'm *that* dad.)

- **The all-time high:** I remember celebrating my birthday with my wife and kids while eating dinner at the small dining table in the RV (parked on the beach in Destin, Florida). We had driven from Disney World the day before. We spent my actual birthday lounging and playing on the beach. My wife made a lopsided chocolate cake in the tiny oven and crammed it full of cheap birthday candles. My kids sang to me. It was on the final leg of our trip, and I have never felt a greater sense of calm togetherness with my family and achievement for creating a true family adventure.

- **The end:** I remember returning home, sad to be at the end of our journey, but happy to sleep in my own bed. My wife's parents were waiting for us on our front porch and had decorated the house with big "Welcome Home" banners. And we ate takeout Tex-Mex while recounting our adventures.

So my friend who was curious about the RV trip asked me if I would do it again. And I said, "Absolutely. In a heartbeat." I didn't need to remember every moment of the experience to know that I would happily do it again.

Sounds like a pretty amazing experience, right? And it was. But upon closer inspection, there were many moments during the trip that were not so great. I actually kept a journal during the trip. While writing this book, I went back through that journal and was surprised by some of the terrible moments I had forgotten:

- **July 24—Arrived at our first stop, Hot Springs. Noticed a huge crack forming in the windshield.** *It's the only part of the RV rental not covered by insurance!* Spent the entire next day trying to find someone who could drive to the park and repair it.

- **July 29—Broke down on the Blue Ridge Parkway.** Was riding the brakes too hard. Started to smell smoke, then the RV caught on fire. Pulled off on the side of the road and waited four hours for roadside assistance.

- **August 8—The heat and mosquitoes drove us out of the Everglades.** We've never felt oppressive heat like that. And there was no escaping the mosquitoes. We all had hundreds of mosquito bites and the kids cried all night. So we packed up and left the next morning, two days earlier than expected.

- **August 12—My daughter Bonnie rolled off the top bunk last night and scraped her back on the bunk bed ladder.** We woke up to her shrieks and she cried for two hours while we soothed her to sleep with an ice pack on her back.

These days, we all look back on those low points and laugh. Even though they were genuinely bad moments, we don't dwell on them. In fact, we only think about them when someone brings them up. But why are we able to laugh about them now? We certainly weren't laughing then.

Chip and Dan Heath provide an extensive answer to this question in their book *The Power of Moments.* In short, social science has proved that the human brain is incapable of remembering every moment over the course of a lifetime, or even a single experience like our RV adventure. So the brain groups moments into experiences and tags the experiences with the defining moments to reduce the processing power required to make future decisions based on our memories. So a few low moments don't establish the essential nature or defining characteristics of that experience for me. Nor do the thousands of forgotten moments (good and bad). I would absolutely go on that RV trip again. Why? *Because of the way the trip made me feel about myself and my family based on the defining moments.* And, like most people, the moments I most remember are the beginning, the end, and the peak moments in between.

"What's indisputable," write Heath and Heath, "is that when we assess our experiences, we don't average our minute-by-minute sensations. Rather, we tend to remember flagship moments."

And so it follows suit that perceptions of the quality of time spent with a company (the customer experience) are not forged by the average quality of all moments recorded in real time (even though it feels that way sometimes). The lasting perception of the customer experience (the essential nature and defining characteristics of the overall experience) is created by the defining moments.

CHAPTER 14

Dedication

For Jennifer. I am grateful for the many defining moments we have shared.

CHAPTER 15

How to Identify Defining Moments

Defining moments typically happen during transitions (the beginning or end of a domain experience) or during moments that we all know are big deals.

The first step in designing defining moments that cement your experience vision in the various domains of customer experience is to identify where your defining moments currently exist. Here is an important fact. Defining moments are already there regardless of whether you're aware of them. If you can't intuitively list the defining moments in your marketing experience (for example), there are probably several reasons why:

- You've never really thought about the concept of defining moments in the context of customer experience, either intuitively or otherwise.

- The relative significance of defining moments in your overall experience is low (in other words, the things that stand out don't really stand out enough to be noticed by the company, but tip the scales of experience in one direction or another nonetheless).

- You don't know where or how to look.

Here are some clues for where to look. Defining moments tend to follow patterns from company to company. Heath and Heath provide some good general guidance that can be applied to tech companies. As relayed above, defining moments typically happen during transitions (the beginning or end of a domain experience) or during moments that we all know are big deals. It's easy to spot most of them in the sales experience. The first contact from a salesperson is a frequent starting point for the sales experience. That's a transition moment from some other domain experience to the sales experience and is thus very likely to be a defining moment. The moment that a prospective customer signs on the dotted line is the ceremonial end of the sales experience, marking the transition from the sales experience to the product experience. There's probably a defining moment for both the sales experience and the product experience in there somewhere. And then there are the big-deal moments like the demo and the proposal. These are probably defining moments one way or another. Do they reinforce the quality of the customer experience you're trying to create? Or do they diminish and confuse it?

But frequently, defining moments exist in spots that are not obvious. Perhaps it's because these moments were specifically created with the intent of standing out from everyday moments (even without the context of holistic customer experience), or perhaps they developed organically over time for reasons that no one remembers or can explain.

The Unexpected Defining Moment

As an example, I worked with an employee recognition company many years ago that would go out of the way during every customer visit to collect the jewelry people were wearing, run it back to the shop where they manufactured custom jewelry for service anniversary rewards, polish it to a luster, and return it to the visitors. I asked Pete

Chambers, the company's founder and then-CEO, why they did that. He said he did it for two reasons. First, he wanted to emphasize that he had his own jewelry manufacturing facility in the same building where the development team wrote code and the customer success team worked with customers. Most of his competitors did not manufacture their own service anniversary awards, and he saw that as a competitive advantage. Second, he wanted people to know that his company was filled with the kind of people you could trust to disappear with your jewelry for a few minutes and return it in better condition. There is no doubt in my mind that Pete had intuitively created a defining moment that was unique in both its style and its position in the sequence of sales experience moments. And it had a durable impact on customer experience. Years after signing on with Inspirus (acquired by Sodexo in 2016), customers would tell the story of how nervous they were to give up their jewelry and how pleasantly surprised (and relieved) they were when it was returned freshly polished. It sealed the deal!

On the other hand, I worked with a manufacturing software company many years ago where the founder and CEO insisted on personally meeting with prospective customers as soon as they were qualified as sales opportunities. He felt that his position in the company and his passion for the product would demonstrate a deep level of commitment to the customer. Could have been a nice touch. Unfortunately, to most prospective customers, he came off as condescending, off-putting, and generally unlikable. All the salespeople knew it too and tried as best they could to sneak prospective customers through the sales process without the CEO meeting. There were never as many big sales meetings as when the CEO was on vacation!

Through a series of interviews with the sales team and a large sample of win-loss data, we were able to isolate his special meeting as a leading cause of lost deals. This was a different kind of defining moment—an all-time low. A moment that not only stood out as definitively unpleasant, but also contradicted the quality of moments leading up to the special meeting. And this moment was automatically invested with significance because it was created by someone associated with the essential nature and true character of the company—the founder.

Asking Questions

Which brings me to the best method for identifying defining moments. In addition to looking for inherently significant moments like beginnings and endings, and following the patterns of typical big-deal moments in any given domain experience, I always recommend interviewing a large sample of people who have gone through the experience (on all sides). We ask questions like, "What moment do you remember most about your sales experience? How would you describe that moment? How did it shape your overall perception of the company?" Inevitably, when you ask enough people questions like that, you start to see a very clear pattern of defining moments and what they reveal about people's perception of the essential nature and defining characteristics of your company.

Once you have an idea of where the defining moments in your various domain experiences currently exist, you have some decisions to make. Do you want to focus effort on shaping your existing defining moments? Make the all-time-high moments even higher and bring them into alignment with your experience vision? Fix the all-time-low moments by making them go away or by making them yet another mostly forgettable moment in the parade of effective and efficient blocking and tackling moments? Even more ambitious, do you want to turn your all-time lows into all-time highs? This may be necessary if your all-time-low moments occur in spots that are generally considered big-deal moments (like a sales demo). And finally, do you want to create new defining moments that don't follow customer expectations—like the jewelry polishing moment at Inspirus?

You get the idea. So the next step in designing defining moments (after discovering where your current defining moments exist) is to decide which moments in any given domain you will focus on.

Beginnings. Endings. All-time highs. All-time lows. One thing you want to keep in mind is that these defining moments should not be designed as a journey that people go through in a linear fashion where each defining moment builds on the last or *requires* the last for context. Why? Because as we've discussed, the customer experience is not a linear journey. What about the people who are invited to the sales demo (in our ongoing example of the sales experience) but were not part of the first sales meeting? Defining moments have to stand on their own and stand out based on their quality relative to similar moments in other companies (but at the very least, your competitors).

CHAPTER 16

Breaking the Script

Of all the concepts that contribute to the design of defining moments, none are more important than breaking the script.

Now that you know the moments you want to focus on, how do you make them true defining moments that bolster the desired quality of your customer experience and drive breakthrough results? One of the non-negotiable components of a defining moment is that it must deliver on your experience vision, not just promise it. It has to pass your own experience design test. Let's revisit the example of The Starr Conspiracy's experience vision. The essential nature of our customer experience is abundance and the defining characteristics are thinking big, sharing freely, focusing on opportunities, and demonstrating gratitude. So when we design defining moments for ourselves, the moment must deliver on our experience vision by passing the *abundance test*:

- Does it bring big ideas to the table?
- Are we sharing freely?
- Are we focusing on opportunities?
- Are we demonstrating gratitude?

Any idea or concept for a defining moment that does not pass the *abundance test* must be discarded lest we accidentally create a defining moment that gives off the wrong impression of who we truly want to be.

There are multiple other design techniques that can contribute to the successful creation of a defining moment. A few of these include investing the moment with heightened significance, promoting a sense of pride, and deepening connections. But it's probably easiest to ask, "How do we make this feel special?"

No matter what, the moment you create is not a defining moment unless people notice it! And so, the real secret to creating a defining moment is breaking the script. *You have to break the script.* Repeat after me. Break. The. Script.

Of all the concepts that contribute to the design of defining moments—the kind that *deliver* your desired customer experience and drive breakthrough results—none are more important than breaking the script. We must all learn to break the script. And let me tell you, it's not easy.

I want to spend some time on the concept of breaking the script because it is frequently misunderstood. What is a script and how do you break it? Often, when I talk about breaking the script, especially in the context of advancing beyond blocking and tackling in sales and marketing, people assume that what I'm talking about is the script that we all follow when we're designing brand, marketing, or sales campaigns. You know, there is a script for how a website should be designed. There is a script for how nurture campaigns are supposed to work. A script for display ads. A script for SDR outreach cadences. From this perspective, it's easy to slip into the posture of equating scripts to "best practices." Like when we obsess over the subject lines of email campaigns based on the prevailing best practices that govern such things, aren't we obsessing over the script? As we pursue the ever-elusive goal of performance optimization through endless A/B tests, aren't we pursuing the best of best practices? And here's food for thought: In our endless quest to conform to the latest, most effective best practices, aren't we working at cross-purposes to breakout marketing? Great marketing is supposed to be the quest for something different, right? Then why are we always trying to copy the stuff that other people are doing?

Anyway, this *is* part of what I mean when I talk about breaking the script. But it is an incomplete picture. Most scripts have multiple roles. Exceptions aside, that's the kind of script I'm talking about. The kind where I have my role and you have your role, and as long as I'm following the script, so are you. That's the script that we need to break. In fact, one of the biggest problems with the blocking and tackling era is the notion that we only have to consider our role in the experience. That's a one-person show.

Trick-through Rates

Here's an example from the marketing experience. My role in the script of running a lead nurturing campaign is basically to trick you into opening my email and clicking on something.

Side note: I literally just got off a call with Casey Carey, one of the best strategic marketing people I've worked with in the tech industry. He's currently the CMO at Quantive, a Work Tech company that delivers Objectives and Key Results (OKR) software. When talking about this topic, he told me that he often uses the phrase "trick-through rates" to talk about this script-driven phenomena.

In preparation for my role in the script, I will obsess over best practices for increasing open rates and click rates. I will test subject lines like "Re: Quick Question for You" with the goal of simply getting you to read the first sentence of my email. I will test different opening lines in the email with the goal of getting you to the first hyperlink. Whatever I can do to increase the number of people who click through from 1 in 1,000 to 10 in 1,000, I will do. And if I can increase that click-through rate by just a smidge, I will call it success. That's performance optimization. And even if I'm harming the customer experience for the other 990 people, as long as I'm improving performance, I'm achieving the goals of my role. I'm following the script.

On the other hand, the prospective customer's role in the script is to avoid marketing emails at all costs. If I'm the prospective customer in this script, I wake up every morning, scan my email, and delete 95% without engaging. I'm a heat-seeking missile for marketing emails. I'm looking for any sign that something is *spam* (that dreaded word). Perhaps a repeating pattern in subject lines such as a relatively recent spike in "Re: Quick Question for You." And all the while, I'm learning to spot other patterns and hardening my defenses. A hyperlink here. A bulleted list there. A percentage sign. A bolded headline. Whatever you throw at me, my goal is to swat it down. And that's how I eliminate 95% of my inbox in 10 minutes or less.

As long as the marketer is following the script, the prospective customer is following the script. It's okay to follow the script in certain blocking and tackling contexts (I'll get to that later). But when it comes to creating defining moments? Like the first time someone receives marketing from your company? Following the script is a non-starter.

Scene: The Restaurant

You see, as long as everyone is following the script, no one is really paying attention. How can we expect to create a defining moment if no one is even aware the moment happened?

Take the example of eating in a restaurant. I have a role in that script. But so does the host and the server and the bartender and the manager and literally everyone else in the restaurant.

Bret enters restaurant and approaches host stand.

Host: "Do you have a reservation?"

Me: "Yes. It's under Starr."

Host: "There you are. Right this way."

Walks to table.

Host: "Your server will be right with you."

Server arrives at table.

Server: "How are we doing tonight? Can I get you started with some drinks?"

Me: "I'll have a vodka martini."

Server: "Great. I'll have that right out."

Server places drink order. Bartender makes drink. Server returns to table and describes specials.

Server: "What can I get started for you?"

And so on and so on. Maybe the manager appears in the third act to ask us how everything was. Maybe, near the end, we hem and haw as we decide whether to order dessert. *We always order dessert.*

As long as everyone follows the script, the whole experience seems to run in the background. It's extremely likely that a few days later, I won't remember when and where I ate out last, or what I ordered. And the server will definitely not remember me. We were all following the script.

But if the script is broken? If the server spills a pitcher of cold water down my back, that's a script-breaking moment. A defining moment. And I will likely develop a negative perception of the overall experience based on that single defining moment. If the manager brings me a slice of cake covered with sparklers, puts a sombrero on my head, and sings "Happy Birthday" to me, that's a different script-breaking moment that will establish the essential nature and defining characteristics of my overall customer experience that night in a different way.

If we want to create true defining moments, we have to break the script. Because the primary requirement of a defining moment is that it stands out, evoking both a heightened sense of awareness and emotional sensitivity. *I'm paying attention now, and I'm about to feel something.*

Sales Experience or Marketing Experience?

Let's look at a real example of defining-moment design in the context of sales experience. I recently worked with a company that was struggling to set first meetings. Like many tech vendors, this company had switched to an outbound sales model during the pandemic because inbound leads were no longer generating enough sales opportunities. In fact, conversion rates had declined across the entire sales and marketing process. But in their estimation, it was the dip in first meetings that was causing the most damage. By the time we started working with them, they had a very specific goal—*double first meetings*. Since they had made several failed runs at this objective, we recommended starting with research.

First, we mapped their outbound sales process by interviewing everyone on the sales and marketing teams. Why bother with so many interviews when we could have just asked the sales leader to describe the sales process to us? There are many reasons, but here are two that are extremely relevant to this case: (1) there is always a gap between the theoretical design of the sales process and how it is actually playing out and (2) very small (and often overlooked) aspects of the sales process can often have an outsized impact on results.

This company had a very vanilla outbound sales process (on paper):

1. Identify target account

2. Source qualified prospects

3. Set discovery meeting (first meeting)

4. Conduct demo

5. Deliver proposal

But the way the sales experience was actually playing out was much different. It was chaotic and it bounced between the sales experience and the marketing experience in unexpected ways, as we'll see in a moment. And there was a very small aspect of the sales process that was incredibly significant to the overall perception of performance. Target accounts were not classified as a sales opportunity until the discovery meeting was set. In other words, an SDR could reach out to a target account 100 times asking for a meeting, but it wasn't until a qualified prospect *agreed* to a meeting that the account was designated as a sales opportunity in the CRM. Among other things, this meant that if a qualified prospect agreed to a meeting but didn't show up, the account would be designated as "closed lost."

After mapping the sales process, we took a deep dive into the engagement history of closed deals (both *closed won* and *closed lost*). This was not an easy process as there was no capability in the marketing automation or CRM solutions to rapidly generate a history of all the interactions between the company and the target account. So we painstakingly reviewed the individual interactions for each sales opportunity that had been designated as *closed won* or *closed lost* within the last year. In some cases, this meant reviewing years of previous marketing and sales interactions between different company representatives and different contacts within the accounts. But we got through it.

As a result of carefully reconstructing an engagement history of each closed deal in our sample, we were able to spot some very clear patterns. And these patterns demonstrated that the actual sales process was different from the theoretical sales process in some important ways. For example, *closed won* deals happened like this:

- SDRs identified new target accounts

- SDRs sourced qualified prospects for target accounts

- *Important: For the vast majority of new target accounts and qualified prospects, there was no previous engagement*

- SDRs attempted to set a meeting with qualified contacts via phone, email, and LinkedIn

- *Important: SDRs failed to set a meeting 100% of the time (remember—these are the prospects who eventually became customers!)*

- SDRs abandoned sales pursuit and assigned qualified contacts to lead nurturing
- *Important: Since the qualified contacts never agreed to an initial sales meeting, they were not officially converted to a sales opportunity and therefore were not designated as "closed lost" at this point*
- Over time, qualified contacts engaged with marketing
- Months later (and completely by chance), SDRs once again attempted to set a meeting with qualified contacts
- Qualified contacts accepted a meeting
- Deal closed at high velocity

Since the target accounts in this *closed won* sample were not designated as sales opportunities until the discovery meeting was scheduled, it appeared to sales management that the "sales cycle" was very short following the first meeting. That's what led the company to conclude that more first meetings would solve everything! What is lost in that analysis is the fact that the *sales experience* actually started months prior to the first meeting when the SDRs initially reached out and that prospective customers were bouncing between moments in the sales experience and moments in the marketing experience for a long period of time.

Closed lost deals looked pretty different in some important ways. In most cases, these deals also started with the SDRs identifying the target account, sourcing qualified prospects, and reaching out to schedule a discovery meeting. But the decision to officially start the "sales process" as soon as the prospective customer agreed to a discovery meeting meant that the vast majority of sales opportunities were closed at the first meeting stage. Many prospects didn't show up for the discovery meeting. Others showed up, but were qualified out because they didn't have purchase intent. But what most of the *closed lost* deals had in common was that there was zero engagement prior to the initial outreach by the SDR. An interesting fact (unknown to sales management) is that *closed lost* deals were excluded from future marketing efforts (lest they accidentally find their way into the sales process again).

We gleaned from these patterns that the probability of setting a meeting with *unengaged* target accounts was virtually zero. Where there was no history of previous engagement, there was very little appointment-setting success. Furthermore, unengaged accounts that *did* agree to a first meeting very rarely advanced in the sales process and were shunned once they dropped out. It became very clear that the *marketing experience* following the initial outreach by SDRs was critical to building engagement, and that engagement was critical to advancing in the sales process. But what we couldn't determine was the role of the initial SDR outreach in initiating the engagement-building process. Was the first outreach by SDRs wasted or was it an important step in the *marketing experience?*

We decided to make the assumption that the first outreach was significant to the engagement-building process. Our basis for doing so was the observation that nearly every closed deal we analyzed started with an unsuccessful sales outreach, followed by a slow build of engagement. On the other hand, we didn't see many closed deals where engagement existed prior to the first sales outreach. Nearly every *closed won* deal started with a failed attempt to set a meeting. It wasn't a perfect assumption, but it got us moving in the right direction.

Now we had an interesting challenge. Was that first outreach by SDRs part of a sales experience or part of a marketing experience? Either way, there is a high probability that it's a defining moment, right? It's a transition moment. The beginning of a domain experience. Viewed as a moment in the sales experience, it was uniquely unsuccessful. Efforts to book meetings with unengaged prospective customers were virtually futile. In fact, in nearly all cases, the unengaged qualified contacts were not even opening the sales emails. Viewed as a moment in the marketing experience, there was still no evidence that the actual outreach by SDRs achieved anything. But there was clear evidence that in this sample of *closed won* deals, target accounts did eventually start engaging with marketing campaigns, which became the building blocks of future sales success. Would they have engaged with marketing if they had never been contacted by SDRs? There is no way to know.

We decided to approach the initial outreach to unengaged contacts as a defining moment in the marketing experience rather than the sales experience, and this created all kinds of challenges. First of all, our proposed solution did not immediately meet the client's requirements. They wanted to drive an *immediate* impact on their performance against first meeting goals. We ended up proposing a different initiative to meet that objective. More on that later. Second, we wanted to use the SDRs to help create a defining moment at the front end of the marketing experience. But SDRs were not incentivized to drive marketing outcomes. They were paid to set meetings. Given the choice to spend their time doing something that may drive company goals but that would not immediately help them hit the goals they were paid for, behavioral economics dictates that they would continue pursuing the low-probability outcome of setting meetings with cold prospects and neglect or ignore activities aimed at initiating engagement. Honestly, that makes sense. Incentive plans tell people what to focus on. If they are hitting their personal incentive goals, they should rightfully assume that they must be driving company goals because that's how their incentive plan was designed. Right?

This is a challenge we run up against frequently. There is an obvious value in using SDR-like resources to initiate and accelerate the engagement-building process. But the standard blocking and tackling playbook doesn't have a page for utilizing sales resources to drive marketing outcomes. Different domains, right?

Thankfully, we were able to demonstrate that the probability of setting meetings with target accounts increases significantly when accounts are engaged. And we successfully argued that the SDRs had the skills and capacity to execute programs that would increase the number of engaged target accounts. As a result, the client agreed to incentivize SDRs for some aspect of engagement building, but what would it be? We settled on moving the hypothetical engagement score from zero to one. From absolutely no engagement to a single interaction from a previously unengaged prospective customer. For that outcome, the SDR would earn $10.

Viewed through the lens of defining moments and holistic customer experience, we counterintuitively identified the first contact by an SDR as a defining moment in the marketing experience rather than the sales experience—it's the first time a prospective customer receives a direct message from the company. Our goal for that defining moment became getting as many people as possible to tune in rather than hit the mute button. See how the shift in perspective changed our focus from the very few to the very many? It was no longer about how to get 1 in 100 people to take a meeting. It was about getting all 100 to engage (or, at least, as many of that 100 as possible). Now we had to figure out how to break the script so that the prospective customers wouldn't swat us down.

You know what I'm talking about. If we're all following the script, the marketers (and in this case, the SDRs) will try to trick the customer into engaging with something. Opening an email. Returning a call. Clicking on something. The customer is going to try to swat it down. Classify the marketing campaign as junk so they can get on with their lives. And it's worth pointing out that, in this particular moment, a decision to mute us rather than tune in has far-reaching implications. If they swat down our first attempt, they are likely to keep us on mute for quite a while. That's just the way it is. After having made the decision that the company is not worth hearing from, it gives the prospective customer permission to extend that decision to future contacts.

Here's exactly how we broke the script and created a defining moment. One more time—why is creating defining moments important? Because perceptions about the essential nature and defining characteristics of the company (our customer experience) are mostly formed based on a few moments that stand out from the rest. And why is breaking the script important? Because when we don't break the script, everyone keeps following the script. And the prevailing script in tech marketing is filled with conflict and features a firmly established antagonist (the company) and protagonist (the customer) who are constantly at odds until one or the other wins. But oh the carnage along the way.

The Entire Design Process in a Nutshell

1. Identified Current Defining Moments

Using research that included interviews with marketing and sales representatives, executives, and prospective customers; process mapping; win-loss analysis and pipeline analysis; and engagement history analysis (along with our experience-based knowledge about where defining moments are frequently found across most tech companies), we identified the beginning of the marketing experience (first marketing contact) and the beginning of the sales experience (first sales contact) as the defining moments most relevant to the business goal of increasing first meetings. For what it's worth, we identified other defining moments in marketing (the all-time-high marketing moment and the moment that most often marked the transition from the marketing experience to the sales experience). And we identified other defining moments in sales (the demo and the transition from the sales experience to the product and customer success experiences).

2. Tied the Moment to Experience Vision

When we first started working with this company, they already had a product experience vision: Make it remarkable. We found that this product experience vision was already expanding to other domains. We wanted to build on what was working instead of introducing a whole new existential concept. So we focused on helping the company see the benefits of expanding this vision to all domains of customer experience (and even the other two experience realms: employee experience and shareholder experience). Not surprisingly, the primary benefit was in elevating the sales and marketing strategy and vision beyond blocking and tackling performance optimization. To get there, we workshopped the customer experience framework and then engaged in the heavy lifting of providing more definition for the experience vision and using that vision to give shape to marketing and sales strategies. We answered the question, "What are the defining characteristics of a remarkable experience?" For this company, a remarkable experience was one that **is surprisingly easy**, **delivers unexpected value,** and **is worth talking about.** We then proceeded into the marketing experience design phase focused on creating a defining moment that delivered on this vision.

3. Designed the Moment

We knew that we had to design a moment that would help achieve the business goals *and* firmly establish the experience vision. To only focus on the domain-level quantitative goals was a recipe for temporary success but long-term value destruction. Remember that the initial business goal was to double first meetings—but upon closer inspection, we found that the probability of setting a first meeting in the opening moment of the current sales experience was virtually zero. (We solved that problem, and I'll explain how in a moment.) So we reframed the challenge as a defining moment in the marketing experience rather than the sales experience—the first time a target account receives marketing from the company. Rather than optimizing around a quixotic goal to set meetings with unengaged prospective customers, we optimized around a very achievable goal to establish and accelerate engagement. We knew that building engagement was the most important factor in our ability to set meetings down the road. No engagement? No meeting. So, indirectly, to create a more sustainable sales experience, we focused on the marketing experience to build the raw materials that sales needs (engaged target accounts). And we invested this moment with the experience vision to ensure continuity between different domain-level experiences down the road. To deliver on the experience vision, we explored different concepts that would demonstrate *remarkably easy, unexpected value,* and *worth talking about.* In the end, we settled on a campaign delivered via email, LinkedIn, and phone that required no interaction or response to the company of any kind (remarkably easy) and that delivered unexpected value in the form of a gift. And we made sure that the gift was worth talking about! (Because if they were talking about the gift, they would certainly be talking about where the gift came from.)

4. Broke the Script

We had to break the script. If we didn't, prospective customers would most certainly put our unsolicited contacts on mute. And if they ignored our first contact, we would be on mute for quite some time and that would reduce the overall number of people who become engaged and slow down the engagement-building process (which we identified as being critical to sales success down the road).

In the script, the company is the antagonist, working obsessively to trick people into completing a form or taking a sales meeting. The prospective customer is the protagonist working hard every day to avoid being tricked into engaging with marketers or salespeople. That's a hard script to break!

For this particular defining moment, we partnered with an ABM gifting platform. Among other things, this gifting platform enables salespeople to initiate cadences from their sales execution solution (Outreach in this case) that offer people real gifts delivered via mail (prospective customers claim their gift by entering their shipping information directly into the gifting platform).

For the gift, we settled on one of those big (40-ounce) Stanley cups. Why? Because it was inherently valuable on its own (we did not brand the cup) and it was a frequently discussed product on social media. The gift was a major part of the campaign, intended to deliver unexpected value and to be worth talking about. Of course the creative, copy, and campaign execution across all channels were excellent, but I won't bore you with the details. More than half of qualified contacts engaged to accept the gift! That is huge. Way better than blocking and tackling results. And more importantly, more than half of the recipients chose to tune in rather than mute us (they engaged with follow-on communications). Once the prospective customer had claimed their gift, they received several shipping notifications via email and text that let them know the status of their order. We were able to customize the content in these shipping notifications through the ABM gifting platform, and while we never asked for a meeting or tried to drive any other response or call to action in these shipping notifications, we were able to include significant company message components. And you know what? Everyone opens a shipping notification. I can't say the same about follow-on messages that are nested in a nurture cadence.

And so we achieved our goal of creating a defining moment. The campaign broke the script, resulting in unprecedented engagement. What's more, these qualified contacts were much more likely than others who didn't receive the defining moment campaign to engage with future blocking and tackling marketing emails (because they didn't mute us). So we increased engagement on the front end and accelerated engagement building after the campaign. Some people give me a hard time about the Stanley cup because it cost over $50 per unit. To them I say, "How much do you pay for clicks to drop people on your website?" And the quality of these prospects is much better because they are carefully chosen from a field of actual target accounts. Blocking and tackling approaches create fake rules about when you should and shouldn't use incentives. In my opinion, this is a much better use of incentives and ends up costing less than paid media programs that have a very low conversion rate when focused on high-involvement outcomes.

Oh. And about the first meetings? Three things. First, we were pleasantly surprised by the fact that about 5% of people who received the defining moment campaign actually reached out to request a meeting! (We quadrupled the first meetings from SDR outreach without even trying.) Second, after a six-week period of building engagement, the SDRs reached back out to this group with a different cadence to set meetings and were successful slightly more than 10% of the time (and in the meetings, people went on and on about that damn Stanley cup). Finally, as I mentioned previously, we implemented a separate recommendation for the appointment-setting process—instead of having SDRs pursue cold target accounts with no previous engagement, we focused them on prioritizing target accounts with high levels of engagement from the house list. The results represent a complete turnaround of the SDR function based on both engagement-building and appointment-setting success.

You know what we're working on now? This is true. I'm not making this up. They're fielding too many meeting requests for their small SDR team. So we're trying to figure out whether it makes more sense to grow the team or down-pace our engagement-building efforts, targeting a smaller universe of more qualified target accounts. Boom.

CHAPTER 17

The Connect/Convert Trap

The connect/convert model is a slash-and-burn model. It creates the worst customer experience for the most number of people, but yields just enough success with the relatively small group of people who survive the slashing and burning that companies keep running it.

Now that we have established a baseline for the three components of The Starr Conspiracy customer experience framework, I want to finish with three topics:

- **The connect/convert trap**
- **The interdependence of experience vision and domain strategy** (e.g., brand strategy, marketing strategy, etc.)
- **The transformative power of customer experience applied to blocking and tackling**

Let's start with the connect/convert trap. What is it and how do you avoid it? And why are we even talking about it? What does it have to do with a holistic customer experience? Well, I'll tell you.

The connect/convert trap is a direct outcome of the blocking and tackling era. It is caused entirely by prevailing linear revenue-generation models that underpin contemporary martech and sales tech stacks and the playbooks promoted by these vendors as well as the users trained in their systems and the environments they have created. A holistic approach to customer experience renders the problems caused by the connect/convert trap absolutely obvious because of the breaks in experience continuity the model creates and the destructive impact on the vast majority of prospective customers who come into contact with your company. So I'm writing about the connect/convert trap for two reasons: (1) unwinding connect/convert models represents a huge, immediate opportunity for tech companies and (2) the solution to the connect/convert trap definitively illustrates the problems caused by the blocking and tackling era and the restorative power of a holistic customer experience.

I'll provide an overview of the connect/convert trap now. But I want to make something very clear. I'm only going to scratch the surface of the problems caused by the connect/convert model. In truth, it's even more devastating in even more ways than I am able to cover in this chapter.

Most companies have a two-motion strategy for revenue generation (even when they say they don't):

- Connect

- Convert

These two motions are stretched across brand, marketing, and sales (but rarely product and customer success). In short, most companies seek to **connect** with qualified contacts and **convert** them into customers. When viewed through the lens of a holistic customer experience, the impact on the five domains looks something like this:

- **Brand Experience**—Executives say, "What is the ROI of brand initiatives?" And that's code for, "Where are the leads?" Most tech companies don't really understand the goals of the brand experience (recognition, functional association, and brand attributes). And there is even less understanding of (or belief in) the influence these brand goals have on outcomes in every other domain of customer experience and on business performance. Therefore, since the impact of brand performance on the connect motion is difficult to quantify (at least with our current blocking and tackling), most tech companies only dabble in brand experience and instead concentrate most marketing resources on lead generation.

- **Marketing Experience**—Executives say, "We need marketing to drive qualified leads." The role of engagement is rarely, if ever, considered in marketing due to the always-urgent need for new leads in service of the connect function. Marketing ends up spending most of their resources on paid, earned, and owned media campaigns with a very narrow focus to connect, connect, connect. And at the first sign of life, these new connections are rushed to sales for the convert motion.

- **Sales Experience**—Executives say: "We need first meetings, demos, proposals, and closed deals." It's a numbers game. And nothing else matters. That's why most tech companies close "opportunities" as won, lost, or no decision starting as early as the first-meeting stage. Because you either bought from me, or you're dead to me. The sales experience in these environments lives in direct service of the convert motion, and the organizing principle for prioritization is typically purchase intent. And when marketing is not getting the connect motion done to the satisfaction of sales, they will usually take it over themselves with an outbound SDR function. Because in the connect/convert model, the only thing sales wants or needs are qualified leads with purchase intent.

- **Product Experience**—Executives say, "We're losing deals because we don't have feature X." In other words, the product experience is not seen in the holistic context of customer experience. Rather, product is viewed either as a catalyst or obstacle to the convert motion. The more aggressive the connect/convert model, the more whipsawed the product function ends up being. This is not to say that products should not follow market requirements. It's simply to point out that the connect/convert model often confuses market requirements with sales and marketing requirements. I've outlined several examples in this book where decisions in the marketing and sales domains actually created false signals about market trends and requirements.

- **Customer Success**—Executives say, "We need customer success to increase customer satisfaction and retention." But there is rarely much thought given to whether customers are capable of being satisfied based on the expectations that were set in the fast and aggressive sweep of the connect/convert model. And so customer success becomes a triage function with high employee turnover and customer churn.

A better model for revenue generation utilizes four *distinct* motions:

- Connect
- *Engage*
- Convert
- *Expand*

I could write a whole book on this topic alone. But I'll try to be succinct here. The connect/convert model is a slash-and-burn model. *It creates the worst customer experience for the most number of people, but yields just enough success with the relatively small group of people who survive the slashing and burning that companies keep running it.* The connect/convert model also keeps surviving because it maps directly to our prevailing blocking and tackling. Think about it. Who is responsible for connecting with target accounts and qualified contacts? Mostly marketing. And we have tons of blocking and tackling for that. We know how to drive leads. We know how to acquire lists of target accounts and qualified contacts. How to source contact information. How to convert website visitors. How to scan badges at the trade show. Copy and creative best practices. Incentive best practices. Access to over 10,000 martech solutions.

We also have tons of connect blocking and tackling for SDRs on the sales side. We know how to source target accounts and qualified contacts. How to source contact information. How to set up cadences in Outreach or Salesloft. Email best practices. LinkedIn best practices. Best practices for calling. And so much technology, we often forget to use what we have.

And when it comes to the abundant blocking and tackling for the convert motion in sales? I mean—where do I even start?

But what about the engage motion? Now, most people will theoretically agree that building engagement is super-important. And many may also claim that they have made deep investments in the engage motion. But do our actions prove it? Let's walk that dog.

How about we start by defining engagement? Most companies will generally define engagement as something like the sum of interactions with marketing content. The more things you open. The more things you click on. The more forms you complete. The more engaged you are! But is that really engagement? I don't think so. At best, that is a crude way to measure engagement. And while it may be the best available way for companies to gather information, we all know intuitively that engagement means something more than the sum of interactions with our company.

For example, I'm a big reader. I always have a few books going at once. There is always one on my nightstand, one in the living room, and one at the office. Why do I usually have at least three books going at a time? I would love for you to think it's because I'm so smart that I simply must read more than one book at a time (because only people of average intelligence read only one book at a time). The truth is less obnoxious, but equally as weird. I often lose interest in books, but I refuse to stop reading them until I get to the end. It's a thing with me. I may pick up the books I've lost interest in frequently, but does that mean I'm engaged in the book? No. It means that I can only read so much of it at a time, so I keep putting it down and picking it back up again. You know what it looks like when I'm actually engaged in a book? I can't put it down. I can't stop talking about it. And I won't stop talking about it until everyone around me has read it too.

So doesn't it make sense to define engagement in revenue generation as something other than the sum of interactions with marketing content? Again, maybe that's the best you can do with the systems you have.

But wait a minute. Wait just a proof-is-in-the-pudding minute.

If you were really invested in the notion of engagement, would you settle for systems that don't address the fundamental goal of the motion? It would be absolutely ludicrous to keep systems for the connect or convert motions that do not adequately address the fundamentals of connecting with prospective customers and converting them to closed deals. But most of us have systems in marketing and sales that barely meet our requirements (if they do at all) for understanding engagement levels in target accounts and with qualified contacts, not to mention actually hanging actions off engagement. *Authentic engagement. Like a good book.* People who actually read every article we put out (not just click through to it). People who read the same article several times. Who send it to other folks because they think it's so good or important. Who advocate for our brands on social media. Who attend every virtual event. Who call us to ask questions. Who email us to share their insights. These are the people who are truly engaged. Do we have all the blocking and tackling in place to make that happen, or even to know when it's happening?

And how are you building engagement? Nurture streams? How many of those nurture campaigns are actually focused on deepening relationships as opposed to pulling people further down the funnel? And when people actually engage with your content, does that register as an opportunity to build even more engagement or does it become a trigger for sales outreach to drive conversion?

But I hear you saying, "Not us—we're an ABM shop. We truly get engagement." Well I'm sure this doesn't describe your company, but nearly every single ABM initiative that I've seen is not an ABM initiative at all. Here's what I encounter most of the time when evaluating companies' ABM programs. They all start with the best intentions. *We're going to create a very targeted list of accounts. We're going to focus on reaching as many qualified contacts within these target accounts as possible. We're going to focus on building engagement with these qualified contacts and when we're confident that we have reached the appropriate level of engagement, or when purchase intent has developed with an engaged account, only then will we seek to convert them to a sales opportunity.*

But here's what actually happens. *We started by building a very targeted list of accounts. We wanted to include as many contacts within those accounts as possible, but ended up really focused on economic buyers and direct purchase influencers. We started by focusing on engagement building, but people (sales and executives) became impatient and started demanding qualified leads. Sales started reaching out to our unengaged target accounts and got frustrated because most of the contacts were unresponsive, and those who were responsive had no purchase intent. So we expanded our list of target accounts focused on prioritizing new accounts with purchase intent. But most of the unengaged accounts with purchase intent were either not responsive or were already committed to a competitor. We kept arguing for the model and for the importance of engagement building, but there was just no patience for it. Long story short, sales and management lost confidence in our ABM strategy, so we reallocated the budget to lead generation and outbound sales.*

Sound familiar? Here's something I know to be true (and I bet you know it too). People with high purchase intent but low engagement buy from someone else. So if any system you have is tuned to purchase intent *without considering the role of engagement*, it's doomed to drive your conversion rates down over time. I would rather build my blocking and tackling around people who have high engagement and zero purchase intent—because when they do decide to buy, they'll buy from my company. Of course, it's always great to optimize around target accounts with both high levels of purchase intent and engagement. *But where am I going to find accounts like that?* Oh yeah—I have to make them. But my current blocking and tackling can't help me do that.

The missing element in this ABM example is a genuine focus on the engage motion. ABM doesn't work without it. (And calling it ABX doesn't fix anything.) Unfortunately, building engagement takes time, patience, money, and *the right blocking and tackling to support the engage motion.* The right people, processes, and technology.

Nonetheless, the engage motion is critical to all sales and marketing initiatives. And yet it's always underserved. I'll give you another very simple example. Everyone knows that the good-old-fashioned webinar is a high-engagement affair. Everyone also knows that only about 40% of people who sign up for a webinar actually attend. And everyone knows that calling people a few days before the webinar (to remind them and encourage them to attend) increases the attendance rate to about 60%. So why isn't anyone doing it? Because it isn't resourced. It's a common missed opportunity. Marketing often gets excited about partnering with SDRs to make engagement-oriented calls like these. And sales will often agree. But at the end of the day, SDRs are not incentivized to build engagement. They are incentivized to set meetings. So if they actually get around to making the calls (which they rarely do), we shouldn't be surprised if they immediately slip into the connect/convert mentality and use that call to try and set a meeting! (Which can be incredibly harmful to the engagement-building process.)

I could go on and on about this topic, but the bottom line is that the engage motion is fundamental to revenue generation but hardly ever part of the blocking and tackling. It's likely that what's needed is a new type of role, like an account development representative (ADR) who is incentivized to engage rather than convert. But I've made that pitch dozens of times and haven't seen a single company implement it.

And by the way, this is one of the major reasons why conversion rates have been structurally declining across the tech sector for years. The more we focus on performance optimization tied to the connect/

convert model, the more we harm the engagement-building process that is critical to long-term revenue generation success. Even our intuitive grasp of the role of engagement has been lost in the mania of performance optimizations to our conventional blocking and tackling. All of this could be avoided with a holistic approach to customer experience. With such a perspective, the damage caused by the connect/convert model would become clear.

Generally speaking, I could go on a similar diatribe about the expand motion. But I won't. Companies tend to do a little better on the expand motion than they do on the engage motion, but the blocking and tackling for the expand motion is woefully under-resourced in similar ways. For example, do your customer success representatives have their own seat in the CRM and are they outfitted with expand cadences?

The big picture here is that everyone intuitively understands that the connect/engage/convert/expand model is better than connect/convert. But the lack of resources for the engage and expand motions is not fully grasped until viewed through the lens of holistic customer experience. And besides, the blocking and tackling in most companies is simply not set up to support a four-motion model. So what's to be done? Well. You have to tune your blocking and tackling to support a holistic approach to customer experience.

CHAPTER 18

The Interdependence of Experience Vision and Domain Strategy

Without an experience vision, we often find ourselves in the position of creating programs that drive the metrics-based goals of the domain but fail to consider the broader impact on the customer experience.

These days, people frequently ask me about the strategic goals of each experience domain. In particular, they ask me about the relationship between the experience vision and the strategy for each domain. So I thought I would ease toward the conclusion by summarizing the goals of each experience domain. In doing so, I hope you can see that in order to achieve strategic goals, it is absolutely necessary to take control of your customer experience, create defining moments, and tune your blocking and tackling.

First, I want to be very clear that the experience vision does not replace the strategy for each domain. It shapes it. It adds another dimension—a dimension that becomes incredibly helpful in guiding the design of all the programs that are necessary to achieve the strategic goals of that domain. Without the experience vision, we often find ourselves in the position of creating programs that drive the metrics-based goals of the domain but fail to consider the broader impact on the customer experience. A "great" marketing campaign may drive a 5% response rate and fill the sales team's bucket with MQLs. But what about the other 95%? Are we willing to damage the customer experience for so many just to hit our numbers? Sadly, in most cases, the answer is yes.

Take the brand experience, for example. The strategic goal of the brand experience is not only to communicate the experience vision. Nor is the strategic goal of the brand experience only to build awareness. There is no single strategic goal for brand experience. In fact, the primary strategic goals of the brand experience are to build brand recognition, functional association, and brand attributes (who we are, what we do, and what we're like). But don't you think it's possible to achieve a high level of brand recognition and functional association (hit our numbers) but totally fail with regard to our ability to establish our brand attributes in the mind of the customer? Taken further, don't you think it's possible to succeed in building high levels of awareness but totally destroy our brand along the way? Of course it is. That's what happens when quantitative goals become the surrogates for holistic strategy.

In pursuit of brand goals, and without a clear understanding of the quality of customer experience we want to create, we often struggle to hit the right note with our brand campaigns. With effective and efficient blocking and tackling in brand experience, people may become aware of who we are and what we do, and maybe even what we're like. But how will they come to understand the essential nature and defining characteristics of the experience they will have with us in every moment? And how can we make sure that the perceptions they form in the brand experience line up with their marketing, sales, product, and customer success experiences so that we avoid breaks in continuity that cause lapses of trust? Or that simply leave people thinking, *They are not the company I thought they were.* That's where the experience vision can provide a dimension to our blocking and tackling that simply makes everything we do much more successful. If we hold our brand, marketing, and sales strategies to the rigorous standard of delivering on our customer experience, we can succeed not only in building awareness, driving leads, and closing deals, but also in shaping perceptions pursuant to building long-term, sustainable vendor preference.

With all that being said, here are the primary strategic goals of each domain along with some notes. But keep in mind that moments in these domains must be designed to not only hit strategic goals, but also to reinforce perceptions of the customer experience. And remember that our best tools for shaping perceptions are the defining moments for each domain.

- **Brand Experience**—*Build brand recognition, functional association, and brand attribute recognition.* The brand experience is not about driving leads—it's about shaping perceptions of your brand. The brand experience mostly occurs in contexts where there is no expectation for a direct channel of communication between the customer and the company (e.g., radio, television, outdoor, print, etc.) or where the ability to control the interaction at scale does not exist (e.g., word of mouth, chance meetings with company representatives, earned media, etc.). Brand performance has a positive impact on marketing and sales performance; response rates are higher for companies with more brand recognition, for example. Brand recognition is also predictive of market share. In other words, brands with the highest recognition also develop the most market share relative to competitors in the same field.

- **Marketing Experience**—*Connect with target accounts and qualified contacts. Build engagement. Create purchase intent.* It's not a strategic goal of marketing to identify purchase intent. Rather, it is a goal to create purchase intent, which can only be achieved through engagement. Purchase intent without engagement results in poor downstream performance, so the organizing principle of the marketing experience should be engagement rather than conversion.

- **Sales Experience**—*Create and convert purchase intent.* As a cautionary note, when the sales experience focuses on creating or converting purchase intent with accounts that are not engaged, conversion rates suffer dramatically. SDRs should mostly be applied to initiatives aimed at accounts where engagement is high. If they are focused on the connect motion (connecting with cold target accounts), their focus should shift to building engagement rather than creating and converting purchase intent. Or better yet, you should create a new group of account development representatives (ADRs) focused exclusively on the engage motion.

- **Product Experience**—*Engage customers. Expand use.* The primary goal of any B2B tech product should be to drive deep customer engagement. In other words, it's not enough that customers simply use your product. We want them to use it frequently and for long stretches of time. In most cases, metrics such as average sessions per user and average session duration correlate with NPS and other customer satisfaction metrics.

- **Customer Success**—*Retain customers. Increase lifetime value. Expand product use.* Customer success should own the expand function. People can really get wrapped around the axle when defining customer success goals, but the bottom line is that it comes down to retaining customers by solving their issues and expanding their use of the product, and increasing revenue by getting them to renew and buy other products. I often hear customer success leaders and other executives say that being responsible for account expansion deteriorates their position as trusted advisors to the client. Do you know why they say that? Because the blocking and tackling for the expand motion is not as pervasive and standardized as what we find in the connect and convert motions.

This list is a very blocking and tackling view of the strategic goals for each domain of customer experience. And the blocking and tackling part is incredibly important! (Especially for areas that are underserved like the engage motion in marketing experience and the expand motion in customer success.) But endless performance optimizations based only on these strategic goals do not deliver breakthrough results or cement competitive advantage. If you want those outcomes, implement a holistic customer experience model, enrich your strategic goals with the extra dimension of customer experience vision, and design your defining moments.

CHAPTER 19

The Transformative Power of Customer Experience Applied to Blocking and Tackling

Thank you.

I want to thank you from the bottom of my heart. You read my book! As Max Fischer says in *Rushmore*, "Oh my God! I wrote a hit play! [pauses] And I'm in love with you." Taking the time to read my book means more to me than you'll ever know. I mean it. I turned 50 this year (can you believe it?) and I frequently find myself reflecting on my time with The Starr Conspiracy. I founded the agency more than 20 years ago and it has been a constant source of abundance for me, my family, my partners, and hundreds of employees over the years. It's pretty overwhelming for me to say that out loud. I'm one of the luckiest people in the world. And I have people like you to thank for it. People who are always on the hunt for big ideas. I hope I delivered at least one or two for you in this book.

But my gratitude for you and this industry also compels me to sound the alarm because I sense that we are facing a collective threat. And I feel like I can do something about it. And that's what I hope to achieve with this book. From my perch at The Starr Conspiracy, I can see the steady decline of sales and marketing performance across hundreds of tech companies. And I'm pretty sure that I know why it's happening and what to do about it. And that's what I wanted to share with you.

Sales and marketing results are eroding across the board. You are not alone. Why is it happening? Because great blocking and tackling is no longer enough to win. Everyone has it. And what's worse is that we have all learned the bad habit of aiming for the greatly diminished quantitative goals that feed our beautiful sales and marketing machines. Rather, we should be challenging the prevailing models, envisioning dramatically different approaches, and setting outrageously higher goals. We're all caught in a self-referencing loop that gets smaller and smaller over time.

But we don't have to blow everything up. We all have truly amazing blocking and tackling to build on. When I think back to what was available in terms of people, processes, and technology when I first entered the field of tech marketing back in 1997, I'm more than a little amazed at the incredible innovation over such a short period of time. Back then, I was sending fax blasts, licking stamps, and dropping floppy disks in the mail. Pretty crazy.

No, we don't need to destroy our blocking and tackling. But we need to energize our efforts with carefully designed defining moments that restore performance in sales and marketing. In my heart, I truly believe that infusing your blocking and tackling with a holistic approach to customer experience will change everything. I know it will. I've seen it happen. And given my history in this market and my deep sense of gratitude for all the abundance that has flowed my way through The Starr Conspiracy, I wouldn't say so if I didn't believe it.

Adding a holistic approach to customer experience on top of your existing blocking and tackling will transform your revenue generation results. You'll start to see old challenges in new ways. You'll stop holding your future results hostage to your current need for pipeline fodder. And you'll find a competitive seam that only grows over time.

It all starts with a terrifying decision to stop doing the same things that everyone else is doing and try something new.

Thank you.

END

Acknowledgments

No one writes a book on their own. Even when they write it alone! Take *this* book, for example. One Saturday morning in May, I went up to the office to draft a short article for the company newsletter—but I didn't stop writing until early Monday morning. I didn't eat. I didn't sleep. I didn't answer my phone. I never left the office. And when the writing stopped, I had a book. (A first draft, anyway.)

But even in this extreme example of an unexpected and isolated creative storm—even though I was totally *alone* and hadn't planned to write this book in the first place (at least not yet)—I didn't write it *on my own*. Before I ever sat down to write, while I was writing, and after the writing was done, there were people who might as well have been in the room with me during that weekend in May because, without them, this book would not exist.

This is a book of ideas. And all of my ideas come from working with clients. I am deeply grateful for the thousands of people who have hired my agency, The Starr Conspiracy, over the last 25 years or so. If you are a current or former client, I want to thank you from the bottom of my heart. Not only have you put food on my table for most of my adult life, but you have also created abundance for hundreds of current and former employees. I especially want to thank our clients who stuck with us during the most difficult and uncertain moments of the pandemic. It mattered. Thank you.

I am also grateful for the people I've worked with at The Starr Conspiracy. I have shared many defining moments with my current and former colleagues. During company meetings, I used to joke that if there were ever a zombie apocalypse, these are the people I would want to face it with. After having gone through something like a zombie apocalypse from 2020 to 2023, I can officially report that I was right. I am surrounded by the best people in the world. If you ever worked at The Starr Conspiracy, I am grateful for the time we spent together, for the knowledge you generously shared, and for the big ideas you brought to the table. Thank you.

Without The Starr Conspiracy, there would be no *Humble Guide;* and without Dan McCarron, Kevin Mangum, and Steve Smith (my business partners), there would be no Starr Conspiracy. What if every day running a business felt like hanging out with your best friends? Well, thanks to Dan, Kevin, and Steve, that's pretty much my life. Thank you, Partners. Your voices were in my head the entire time I was writing this book. (I *think* those were your voices.)

My senior leadership team (including the partners), got us through the pandemic. We bent, but we didn't break. I'll die proud of how we treated people when shit got real. Seriously—the abundance you created for others during the toughest of times will echo through generations. Thank you Ashley Bernard, Erin Swan, Jonathan Goodman, Dan, Kevin, and Steve.

Lance Haun came up with the title—pretty funny, I think. Also, the original title was pretty bad: *Why Your Sales and Marketing Shit Is Broken*. But it was Jonathan who demanded a new title in the first place. Also, Jonathan read the book multiple times, provided generous feedback, and suggested several other books and articles (as he does) that helped sharpen some of the big ideas in this book.

Patrick (Pat) Manzo was the first person outside The Starr Conspiracy to read the manuscript. He was kind enough to say it was great while also pointing out all of the reasons it sucked. Also among the first readers were Rob Catalano and Nadir Ebrahim, who know me well enough to give it to me straight (especially Rob, who still owes me a hockey game). And among the handful of advance readers (a really big ask), I also wish to express my gratitude to Jessica Cash, who suggested that I write more about brand.

Speaking of brand, Nancy Crabb demanded an entire chapter on the subject. And since I live in fear of her (she's a pyromaniac), I obliged. Nancy leads the creative team at The Starr Conspiracy and so now is the perfect time to thank Erin Sanders, who designed the cover (ask her about chaos theory). Racheal Bates and Joanna Castle led the marketing and publicity team for the book. Dana Karpinski was the producer (for all print, audio, and video versions)—a natural choice since she has done such a fine job producing my podcasts from the very start! Aaron Delgaty was also a generous advance reader. Thank you all.

Henry Albrecht, Mike Carden, and Julie Knight are heroes of mine. Truly. Imagine my surprise and delight when they not only read the original manuscript, providing me with priceless feedback, but also offered praise for the book! *My* words cannot express the depth of my gratitude for *your* words. Thank you Henry, Mike, and Julie. For everything.

Every moment I've spent working on this book, and, indeed, every moment I've spent working all these years, is a moment I haven't spent with my wife, daughter, and son. I love you, Jennifer. I love you, Bonnie. I love you, Jack. Thank you for giving me a sense of purpose so profound that I sometimes get carried away. And I hope you know, of all the moments I've ever experienced, none come close to the ones I've shared with you.

It's just like Floyd Tillman sang all those years ago.

I love you so much it hurts me so.

www.ingramcontent.com/pod-product-compliance
Lightning Source LLC
Chambersburg PA
CBHW022108210326
41521CB00030B/402